10 PRINCIPLE ⋮E

THE
DAILY
CLIMB

MATT HULLANDER

TABLE OF CONTENTS

DEDICATION

*To my late grandfather William "Troy" Hullander.
He was a good-looking, charismatic fellow. He was part
Cherokee Indian, a farmer, a boxer, a businessman,
and someone who was always caring and lending a
hand any time it was needed. He was an influencer
in his time, and the coolest dude I've ever known.*

This is for you.

ACKNOWLEDGMENT

There are so many to thank. First, I'm enormously grateful to my loving and gracious God. I've been blessed beyond measure with wonderful moments and relationships that help mold me along the way. Next, to my wife Jenny and my daughter Reese. Thanks for your constant love and support. Additional thanks to my parents, anyone referenced in this book, my guides, my tribe, my mentors, my publisher, my incredible friends and all those people that pay if forward and change the lives of others. And last, I would like to thank Matt Hullander (that's me) for not giving up on his dream of writing a book. #makeitbetter #keepclimbing

FOREWORD

In 2012, I had just been fired from the University of Tennessee after 16 years, no violations, a National Championship, 2 SEC championships, 5 divisional championships, and winning 100 more games than I lost, and a soon-to-be first ballot Hall of Famer.

So to say I was not happy with some people at UT would be an understatement. I was really struggling to decide: do I stay in coaching, probably at a place that my family did not love like we loved Tennessee? Do I disrupt my loving and loyal wife and children, to coach somewhere that hasn't won in 50 years? I made the decision to go the coaches' convention, put a staff together, and see what happened.

RC Slocum was a great coach at Texas A&M and a great friend. He had a similar end to his career, like me, and it made no sense in his situation either. He had a great run at A&M, won lots of games, and did it the right way.

I ran into RC in the hallway of the Opryland Hotel on my way to meet with a coach. RC asked me to grab a coffee with him. He said, "I have been looking for you."

He asked the waitress for change for a dollar in pennies. She brought us coffee and a roll of change. RC broke the pennies open and spread them on the table. He asked how old I was... I said 58.

He took 58 pennies off the table.

He said, "Let's say you live to be 85."
Yep. He took 15 pennies off the table. I could see where this was going.
He said, "Those last 5 years aren't going to be great..."
He took 5 more off the table. There we not a lot of pennies left at this point.

He looked me dead in the eye and said, "It is important to count your pennies, but it is much more important to make your pennies count."

Wow! How strong was that?

I decided that day that my wife, children, and grandchildren were the most important thing in the world, and my pennies would be used up on them.

When I was asked by Matt Hullander to do the foreword for his book, I was naturally honored. I do not take it lightly that a great friend has trusted me to publicly endorse his hard work, the sharing of personal, family, and work stories and experiences, and pretty much baring his soul in print.

In this book, Matt asks us to rethink how we are motivated about life, family, and work, as he shares his experiences and insights on his "Daily Climb." Matt encourages us all to work to be successful, but makes us think about defining what success is for each of us personally.

I know Matt. He loves his family, he loves his friends, he is a good man, and Matt will also tell you straight-up that he has lots of things he needs to improve. That is true for all of us on our Daily Climbs. If you are perfect in every way, Matt would say, "This book is not for you."

The Daily Climb is not your typical self-help or motivational book.

It will help you think for yourself, and it certainly can be motivational, but it is not typical! Matt has a style that hits you between the eyes with the truth as he sees it. He touches all aspects of life in such a way that you feel that this is your good friend "coaching" you to think and to rethink for yourself as you make life's big and small decisions.

Matt encourages us, through his experiences, and those of his personal and business friends, to really establish priorities in life, how to put family first, and prioritize our greatest resource: our time.

Matt Hullander believes in what he says about accountability, work ethic, and leadership in an organization. He has challenged and supported his team throughout his life and career, and he has asked them to do the same.

I have personally witnessed how he led from the front, pushed from the back, and at the same time allowed and motivated his people to help him build a successful business. They cared about each other, they felt free to disagree if that is what it took to be successful or to do the right thing for a customer.

Matt's success did not come easy; he worked his tail off and used the principals in this book to be successful in business and life. He loves and provides well for his family, he cares for his friends, keeps his faith central in his life, and will go way out of his way to help those in need.

Matt has many strengths, but one of his best is that he can openly critique himself and be willing to adjust to the circumstances as needed.

So, if you don't mind being punched in the nose, scolded a little, and along the way find help for your Daily Climb...

You have to read this book!

– Phillip Fulmer

PRINCIPLE
1

WEAR EXTRA-BIG SHOES

OR

*Shed Your Skin Like A Snake Every Day;
Buy The T-Shirt; The Daily Climb; Human
Being Not Human Doing; Change Your Life*

It was March 2nd, 2014 at the Dolby Theater in Los Angeles, California, in a room full of rich and famous celebrities and artists, that the actor Matthew McConoughey sat on a velvet cushion, sweating bullets.

He'd had a phenomenal career – working in award-winning movies in various genres, from *Dazed and Confused* to *Texas Chainsaw Massacre*. He'd worked with some of the best directors, actors, and actresses in the business, and he'd become a household name. He had a phenomenal career by any metric – except one.

He had never been able to get a nod from the Academy. He had never won – nor been nominated for – an Oscar. And on this night, March 2nd, 2014, he was in the running for Best Actor.

The competition was nothing to shake a stick at, either. Veteran actor Bruce Dern was up for the award as well, and so were the star of *12 Years a Slave*, one of Hollywood's favorites that year, Christian Bale (who'd previously won an Oscar – and he'd been acting since he was five for Pete's sake), and Leonardo DiCaprio – who everyone knew was destined to win an Oscar one of these days.

It was an impressive list, but when Jennifer Lawrence took the stage, it was McConoughey's name on her lips, and in the middle of the shock and commotion, he realized that he needed to give a speech.

The only problem was, he hadn't prepared a speech. That would've been pretentious, he later said. So, after tapping his forehead with his finger a few times to think, he spoke from the heart.

"There are a few things… about three things, to my count, that I need each day. One of them is something to look up to; another is something to look forward to; and another is someone to chase."

God was who he looked up to. Living life with his family was what he looked forward to. But he had a surprising answer for that last item.

"And to my hero – that's who I chase. When I was 15 years old, I had a very important person in my life come to me and say, 'Who's your hero?' ... I said, 'It's me in 10 years.' So I turned 25... that same person comes to me and goes, 'So, are you a hero?' And I was like, 'Not even close! No, no, no.' She said, 'Why?' And I said, 'Because my hero's me at 35.' So, you see, every day of my life... my hero's always 10 years away... That keeps me with somebody to keep on chasing."

Now, some people might think that it's narcissistic, having yourself in 10 years be your hero, but I don't think that is the intent. Surely the man has people he looks up to, learns from, and respects – but looking at life like you're chasing a better version of you? I think that's awfully wise. He's stumbled onto a deep truth about existing, and doing through being.

See, most people wake up with pain in their shitty back, they go to their shitty job, home to their shitty marriage, all graced with their shitty attitude (Sorry, pastor – I couldn't think of a better word than "shitty"). "Change" is an idea floating out there in the ether, but it isn't much of a reality for most people. Most, whether out of ignorance, laziness, apathy, or who knows what else, just don't change very much. That's unfortunate, because life happens to require constant change out of all of us if we want to be successful.

It's a moving target, but we treat it like it's stationary. No wonder we miss so often.

Now, if you're reading this book and you find yourself perfectly happy with your marriage, your health, your finances, your work, your relationships, and your aspirations, then I suppose you'd be alright to set this one down and celebrate your uncanny success with another author. But for the rest of us – and I suspect that's everybody – there's something that we'd like to improve. We want to make more money, have more respect, get along with our spouse better, look better, feel better – whatever it is, it's something. And I'm here at fifty years old finally in a position where I feel like I have some answers and some wisdom to share.

If you're looking for a book to tell you "try harder," pick up a different book, because that isn't what I'm all about. I believe in better. I believe in vision. I believe in prioritized, disciplined, systematized, delegated, and elevated. But I don't believe in trying.

Because trying doesn't work.

"I'm going to try and lose weight."
"I'm trying to be a better spouse."
"I'm trying to stop tobacco."

It's a bunch of nonsense.

Don't believe me? Check out the numbers:

- How many people complete a New Year's Resolution by the end of the year? Google tells me it's perhaps as low as 9%.
- Roughly 90% of people who lose a significant amount of weight eventually gain it back.

So what's the point? If less than 10% of people are keeping their New Year's resolutions and only 10% of people keep off the weight, should we even try?

I guess the idea is to be one of the 10% that actually gets things accomplished. But that means being smart about it.

What is different about the successful? Heck, how did Matthew McConoughey manage to become an Oscar award-winning actor? How can we make positive change successfully?

It is typically at this point that we start talking about goal-setting, so let me share a goal-setting secret with you – and bear with me.

Read through all of this before you go and do it, but take a sheet of paper, and write down your top ten goals in your life. Be specific. Then, take that paper and fold it in half longways, then the other way, and then fold it over one more time. Walk to a coffee shop, find a table that wobbles, and wedge your folded up paper under the side that's sitting high.

Now, maybe the table won't wobble any more. But the whole goal-setting thing? Screw it.

This flies in the face of a hundred years of motivational speakers, wellness books, and self-help gurus, but we know it to be true, don't we? How does it typically go when you tell yourself that you'll drink less alcohol or go to the gym more or read more? Turns out all of that "manifest it into your life" and "affirm it into reality" nonsense was mostly a marketing ploy.

You need vision, but it isn't about goal-setting. You need effort, but it isn't about trying.

It's about being. Chase the better version of you. Get up every day and climb into his boots.

There's one phrase you absolutely never want to hear your doctor say, and I'm not talking about "You owe me money." There's something a fair bit worse than that.

My doctor's a family friend, and so it wasn't too far out of the blue when he called me from his cell phone one day in the fall of 2019. We traded a line or two of small talk – sort of awkwardly, I thought – and then he asked me to come in so he could go over some bloodwork results from a few tests he'd run during my last physical.

Once I was there in one of those blank, white rooms, he didn't event attempt small talk.

"I want you to see an oncologist, Matt."

"An oncologist?" I said, surprised. I almost said, "What happened to talking about my bloodwork?" when it dawned on me.

He opened a folder on his clipboard and showed me a few charts.

"Your neutrophils are low. So are your white blood cells. See, here is where those numbers ought to be-"

I pointed.

"And those are mine?"

He nodded.

I was in disbelief.
"Dr. Volberg, are you saying I have cancer?"

"I can't possibly diagnose something like that right now, but it would be prudent for you to make an appointment with Tennessee Oncology. No sense in worrying before-"

"Cut the crap, Carlton, it's me. Are you saying I have cancer?"

He sighed and shut the folder.

"I don't know, Matt. You might."

You can probably guess, I made that appointment right away, didn't even bother to leave the doctor's office before I was on the phone. When a doctor says the "c" word, you don't mess around.

Things started to happen fast, then. I saw the oncologist. They ordered test after test, and I watched them fill vial after vial with blood. They tested for every virus, genetic anomaly, and toxin they could think of. But the tests didn't yield any results.

It's an odd thing, hoping for a test to say there's something wrong with you, just so you know that thing isn't cancer. But the tests didn't give us anything, so they did an ultrasound of my organs, and that gave us a clue.

I had an enlarged spleen. I already knew about my existing arthritis. When you put those two things together with the low neutrophil levels, it was starting to sound like Leukemia was the prime suspect. Bone cancer.

They scheduled me for a bone marrow biopsy.

I'd been in too much shock to think about my situation too deeply up till this point, but once Leukemia was on the table, I got scared. I started googling.

The survival rate was about 65%, but that meant the death rate was 35% - and anyway, the survival rate only meant that people lasted for 5 years after a diagnosis. Some of them died after that, I was sure.

I found out about all the different kinds of Leukemia. Myeloid, lymphatic, Myelomono-something-I-can't-pronounce... And some kinds had really low 5-year survival rates, like 20%.

And so, when the morning came for me to go into the hospital for the biopsy, I didn't want my daughter to know where I was going, or why I wasn't taking her to school that day. She was a Freshman in high school. Fourteen. Just in her second month of four years of boys, books, friendship turmoil, life decisions, college applications, forks in the road – She needed her father. And I knew that she might not have him.

My friend Bobby drove me to the hospital that day, and my wife came up with an excuse to drive my daughter to school. I checked in, dressed in one of those awful, backless hospital gowns, and met the doctor who was going to do the procedure. Nice lady. It was hard for me to notice much about the situation beyond that. It was a blur.

They had to put me under for the procedure, so when I woke up, my wife was there, and the doctor told us that they wouldn't have the results of the test right away, which would allow them to know conclusively if I had cancer or not. It would be five days.

How in the hell was I supposed to spend those five days?

They tell you to go home and relax, but that was a joke. I didn't sleep at all. I didn't want to stay home from work because I knew I'd drive myself crazy sitting around, wondering, waiting, pacing. At work, conversations were strained and offbeat, as I tried to dissociate and pretend everything was fine. I tried to distract myself, but in the end, I found I kept spacing out and doing all of that thinking that I was trying so hard not to do.

Did I have cancer? Was I going to die? Chemo and radiation sounded only a little better than torture. And what was the point if so many people went through all that pain and suffering and ended up dying anyway?

I thought about my business, my life's work. I thought about my family. I couldn't imagine not being there for my daughter's wedding day. And how could I ask my wife Jenny to go on without me? She's the love of my life, and I don't want to miss a moment with her. I listened to Tim McGraw's song, "Live Like You Were Dying" over and over.

You see, I've always been a go-getter. I wasn't always successful, but I worked my ass off, and the success came. But working 60, 70 hours a week in a competitive field didn't leave me a lot of time to wrestle with the big questions in life – what my tombstone would say, what my priorities were, who my real friends were, how my relationship with God was, and how much of what I ran around furiously accomplishing really meant anything at all.

But those five days changed my life. Because when you're looking your mortality in the eye, there is nothing else. No distractions to hide you from reflections on your life and legacy.

I won't draw out the ending. Felty's Syndrome was the root cause, and I could live with that. But the most important diagnosis I got, the real results that mattered, told me that I was not someone who was making the most of his life. Things were out of balance. People I loved were getting the short end of the stick. I was using "someday" as code for "never." I didn't enjoy my success, and I lived with a ridiculous amount of stress.

I realized that I had some sorting out to do.

So that's my testimony. My kick in the pants courtesy of life's surprises that sent me on a years-long journey into reorienting my life away from the "palm tree in a hurricane" method, and onto a mode of being that brings me far more fulfillment, peace, and the most important kinds of success. I found out that I could change, and even that I could keep changing a little bit every day.

I ran into an old buddy from high school a couple of weeks back, and in between hearing about the same sports team, the same work, the same gripes, and the same 'poor-me' attitude, I realized that I was looking at a man who hadn't gotten a software update since 1991. I wished he could have an awakening like I had.

So what is it for you? What is that thing that gives you the motivation to live like it's on purpose? To be a better version of yourself a little bit at a time – not through daily affirmations, a rigid system of goal-setting, or any of the latest self-help mumbo jumbo. To acquire a vision of who you could be in 10 years, and to chase that man or woman.

Are you sick of missing out on opportunities? Do you long for some dream that you just never get around to working on? Is there a person in your life, maybe a spouse or a child, who is your motivation for change? Or maybe you got a swift kick to your central nervous system.

Whatever it is, I hope this book will help you envision what your hero is like, equip you with some tried and tested wisdom, and encourage you to get up every morning and put on boots that are bigger than your feet. But maybe they fit just a bit better than yesterday.

That's the daily climb. That's a human being.

PRINCIPLE
2

YOU DON'T STOP
FOR DRY-CLEANING
ON YOUR WAY TO
DIFFUSE A BOMB

OR

Prioritize; Don't Major in the Minors;
Tyranny of the Urgent; SAY NO; Audit Your
Life; What Matters Most

You aren't supposed to start out telling your reader that you aren't very good at something before you explain to them how to do it. That seems, obvious, I suppose. Imagine picking up a how-to book on golf where the first page says, "I, myself, haven't broken a hundred more than maybe once or twice."

I would not advise you to learn about golf from that man.

But at the same time, what not to do can be just as important as what to do, and experience matters when we're talking about life. Hopefully, we understand that in the big lessons, we're all a work in progress.

So, to that end, I'd just like to say that I'm terrible at Principle #2, but I'm getting better, and I've learned a lot in my 50 years. So I'm in the pulpit and the congregation at the same time today. It's less like preaching to the choir and more like preaching to a mirror. But that's enough procrastinating from me.

I've learned that you've got to prioritize.

In the last century, there have been a lot of cool, time-saving gadgets that came out. A nation-wide and international telephone system made a lot of in-person meetings unnecessary and reduced the need for business travel. The fax machine made it so you didn't need to wait on the mail anymore. Typewriters became easier to use and required less maintenance – and then we got computers, laptops, smartphones, and Chat GPT. In the last hundred years, horses have become 500 horsepower engines, digital technology has made information transfer instantaneous, and last I heard, Elon Musk is working on something that lets you access the internet directly from your brain.

Back in the 1930s, people were predicting that, because of all the time-saving inventions, their grandchildren would have 15-hour workweeks. But that isn't what happened, now, is it?

We're busier than ever! Every time I ask a friend how they've been, they say "busy," and I nod and say, "I'm busy too." It's almost a badge of honor. We brag about it. Who's the busiest? Our heroes sleep 4 hours a night and work 20. We've got all of these incredible amenities and technologies at our fingers, but we fill up the time with more hustle, more stress, and more running around.

My father, God bless him, is a hardworking man. Growing up, he managed (and worked on) a farm, ran a business, and worked for someone else as well. He'd be cutting the grass in the dark when he finally got back home at night, and I don't need to tell you there weren't a lot of bedtime stories in the Hullander house. He was sacrificing and busting his hump. Working for his family – but ironically, all of that was stealing time from the family, too.

I'm cut from the same cloth. My story of the not-too-distant past is that I was always in a rush, and heartburn was just a cost of doing business. In less than two years, I sold my business, moved, started and joined several new businesses, built a new home, flew around the world, ran for mayor, lost, and constantly jumped from one thing to the next. My calendar looked like a bathroom door in a rest stop, covered in writing squeezed into all of the margins, turned every which way, with just as many phone numbers – albeit probably with less filthy language.

I lived in a constant hurry, trying to satisfy the next person, grab the next opportunity, to make something happen so people would say "great job!" My flaws were all humble-brags.

I work too hard.

I care too much.

I'm trying to please everybody.

I take on so much.

Truth is, I wanted the bustle so that I'd feel important. I suppose I didn't really think that I was important, and even though the rising profits, the number of people who wanted me on their board, and all external markers of success kept going up, it didn't really fix my basic insecurity. But that didn't stop me from trying. It reminds me of that great line in a country song:

"I tell myself that I should quit [drinking], but I don't listen to drunks."

I was a workaholic. Addicted to a schedule that couldn't let up.

When asked about my priorities, I'd often told others that they were:

1. God
2. My wife
3. My daughter
4. My friends
5. My work

With others, I was painstakingly honest, but with myself, I was a skilled liar. Reality was that my list of priorities was in the complete reverse order.

I mentioned that I ran for mayor, and I'll tell you more about that experience in Principle #8, "Plan to Fail." The title tells you how that race went, doesn't it? Anyway, after that particularly desperate flurry of activity came to an end and I was left to my thoughts and a suddenly-empty schedule, I began to have some clarity.

The only thing I can figure is that God was working in me.

I began to pray more. I thought more about what I would put on my calendar now that I was building it from scratch again. I'd been anticipating meetings with fundraisers, social initiatives, voters, and the like. Turns out people don't ask you to do those things when you aren't the mayor. But the upshot was that in the rebuilding phase of my professional and personal life, I got to redefine what success means to me.

It was a learning process.

It still is a learning process. I'm detoxing from having to be the guy on TV, the guy on the magazine cover, the local celebrity, the guy who ran for mayor, the friend who everybody wanted something from, and the guy everyone knew would deliver.

You see, dad cutting grass outside while I tried to fall asleep taught me something, even though it took me decades to realize it:

You can't "squeeze in" the most important things in life. It is not possible. You can squeeze in a lunch meeting, a little more R&D in the budget, or one extra product launch – but you can't squeeze in peace of mind. You can't "squeeze in" God. He's too big to fit into it anyhow, whatever "it" is. You can't "squeeze in" those fleeting moments in your child's life that happen once and are gone forever.

If you miss it, you miss it. Crops that don't get watered die. People who are in constant motion can't hear themselves think. They certainly can't hear God.

I couldn't hear Him either.

I heard from somewhere that the word "priority" is a very old word, and for the first several hundred years of its use, it was only singular.

"What is *the* priority?"

But after the Industrial Revolution, we started talking about our "priorities." As if by changing language we could make it so more than one goal could be first. It's the old lie of multi-tasking: Nobody really multitasks; we just constantly jump back and forth between tasks, making our quality of work plummet in the process.

The folksy, Southern way of saying this is, "Chase two rabbits; go home hungry." Better to just pick one and give it all you've got.

So in the process of remaking my schedule, re-evaluating how I wanted my work and my life to operate, I had to diagnose how I'd gotten things so ass-backwards. If I said my wife and children were more important to me than my career, why did I spend so many years stumbling in the door to a cold plate of dinner in the microwave, with my kid asleep in bed, and me too mentally exhausted to really connect with my wife? I didn't find myself at church very often, but every time some guy I knew from high school called me in a panic, telling me he needed a fourth for a charity golf tournament, there I'd be, in a golf shirt and a beer, teeing it up and wondering why I was there in the first place.

This is what the gurus call the "tyranny of the urgent." In simpler times, we just said "the squeaky wheel gets the grease." So why doesn't it ever enter our minds that the squeaky wheel is the worst wheel, and maybe the cart would do just fine without it?

It's easy to fly by the seat of your pants, saying yes to everything and killing yourself to make it all work. It's miserable, but easy in the sense that it just sort of happens if you don't stop it.

So I'd at least identified the problem. I had a chronic aversion to an innocent little word:

"No."

See, I thought of "no" as a closed door, a dead end, the death of an opportunity. But time is a fixed resource every day, and everybody gets the same amount. It's a zero-sum game, and so every "no" is a "yes" to something else. You can't cash in your unused time for extra the next day. That makes "no" something good. That makes "no" very powerful.

In the middle of all these realizations, it occurred to me that I was on several boards – I was on the board at a bank, our children's hospital, the chamber of commerce, and three non-profits. What's worse is that I knew I wasn't making an impact on most of these organizations by sitting in a room with sometimes dozens of other people. So I took a hard look at these obligations, and I wrote five resignation letters in one day. I stayed on the one board that I was actively benefitting from and that contributed to my goals. It was difficult to reject the positions of trust and honor that had been offered to me in those other five organizations, but once I did, I was amazed. Suddenly I had more time to pursue my passions, I was more productive in the businesses and organizations I was effective in, and my blood pressure dropped a few points. That's the power of saying no.

You just aren't at your best when you're maxed out all of the time. When do you snap at your loved ones, half-ass it at work, or make a mess of things? It's usually when you're overloaded, and that underlying frustration of values-misalignment haunts you every time you do something that takes away from the truly important things.

I learned to stick to what matters most. "You can have it all!" is a lie. Life is full of little fires that are always popping up, and if you keep turning your attention to whatever "urgent" matter comes up, you'll neglect the things that matter most. You don't stop for laundry on your way to diffuse a bomb.

Ben Franklin said, "Do you love life? Then do not squander time, for that's the stuff it's made of." And let me tell you, we're squandering time left and right.

And that's the really frustrating thing, I guess. Values-misalignment doesn't always come from spending too much time on a board for the local children's hospital where they don't really need you. These days, we've got very stupid ways of wasting our time, and I'm as guilty of it as the next guy, but I'm learning.

You know the average person worldwide spends nearly two and a half hours on social media every day? In the US, the average person spends nearly five hours on their phone daily.

Our marriages are on the rocks, but at least we've seen a lot of cat videos. It'd be funny if it wasn't so damn pathetic.

I have a friend who's an accountant, and he told me something one time that has always stuck with me. He said, "If you aren't selling your business, then you're buying it. So do an audit regularly." It's good advice in business, and it's even better advice for our personal lives. Audits reveal assets and liabilities. It's best to have more assets. If we actually stop to notice and keep track of how we spend our time, it'll give us a really clear picture of how we're doing. You only get one life, so you might as well kick out the things that suck time away from what is good and meaningful.

I'm not saying I don't play golf or have a beer with a buddy. But if I'm doing that, I won't have time for something else, so it's important to keep it all in balance.

People make mistakes. We're all going to stumble and fall – I sure do – but the point is to do better than yesterday.

I'm not kidding myself, and I know I'm not likely to throw my iPhone in the garbage, even if ultimately maybe I should. But I know I can leave that shiny distraction box in the car during dinner on date night. Heck, the best weekend I ever had was fishing in the Bahamas one time when we went out of cell service range for four whole days. Have a docking station at home for your phone, and put it on ring instead of vibrate, so you don't have to carry it with you everywhere you go, constantly tempted to pull it out and scroll. Research suggests that our phones affect our thoughts and behavior whenever they are in the same room with us, even when they aren't turned on.

This isn't a self-help book, so I'm not going to give ten tips for managing your phone or go into details about how you need to master it or it will master you. But I will mention that a large number of Silicone Valley bigwigs pay good money to send their children to "device-free schools" that don't allow personal screens at all.

It isn't all about the phones, though. That's just a symptom. I'm learning to ask myself about the true cost of taking on another responsibility, buying into another company, or even buying another gadget.

There's a book that I greatly appreciate called The Ruthless Elimination of Hurry by John Mark Comer. At one point in the book, he asks you to consider how much things actually cost, beyond their price tag.

Say you want to buy a boat, and it'll be $40,000. You've got the money and you're ready to pull the trigger on the purchase. Great.

But it isn't really going to cost $40,000, is it?

You've got to fill up the gas tank, of course. That's less than the price tag, but it's not nothing.

You'll need to set aside money for repairs and new parts, as you need them. Nothing lasts forever, and if it's mechanical – it'll break down sooner or later.

You'll have to buy some life jackets. Maybe you'll want a stereo system. Some water toys so you can tow water skis or tubes. And you'll have to pay to store it at a marina, most likely – or if you're keeping it in your garage, you'll need to buy a trailer.

And we haven't even mentioned the time investment involved. In the summers, you'll be spending hours and days out on the lake, time planning trips and coordinating with your friends, and time taking a boating license class so that you can drive the thing at all.

The boat costs more than $40,000, and it costs more than money.

Now look, people tell me I'm a fun guy and I'm inclined to agree with them. There's nothing wrong with a boat. A lot of people think heaven is a little closer on a boat on the lake, and again I'd agree. I happen to spend a good amount of time on boats. I'm not against fun – we could do this exercise with something like 'what's the real cost of managing another business?' or 'what's the real cost of taking a second job?'

The point is just that we need to be aware of what we're getting into, whatever it is. Most things come with strings attached, and everything costs something.

Look, I'm just a guy who grew up on a farm in East Tennessee in a small town on a gravel road with no cable television. I lived on the same street for 47 years, come from a great family with terrific parents. I went to the Baptist church every time the door was open, baled hay, mended fences, grew up in the family business, and learned the value of hard work. I educated myself, took out a loan, bought the family business, sought out experts, teamed up with peers, grew the business, and sold it for 8 figures. Now I have interests in dozens of entities ranging from real estate, home services, restaurants, marketing, coffee, dental offices and e-commerce.

Now here's the rub – running one business nearly killed me. Working in a bunch of them is significantly easier. It isn't because there's less work, the business environment is cushier, or because the industries involved are less competitive. None of those things could be further from the truth. I could be busier than ever. But by learning the lessons of prioritizing, I am able to do more with my effort, with less of a headache along the way.

I stick to the essentials.
1. God
2. My Wife
3. My Daughter
4. My Friends
5. My Work

I've got those in the right order most of the time now.

Now I know what many of you are probably thinking:

"How do you have time to run a dozen businesses, but 'work' isn't even your top priority?"

It isn't about "how" to do it. It's about "who" can do it. And the answer to that question is rarely "me."

I think about who I need to help me in all of my endeavors. I think about who I am and who I want to be. At the end of the day, who the heck cares if I built a business all on my own or not? It's the great results that define your success.

This is a big mindset change – more on that in the next chapter – but we have to realize that the team around us and the support we have in our endeavors is how we achieve success. At least, the kind of success that doesn't give you an ulcer. We don't live in solitary confinement, and it's important that we work together to take advantage of our unique strengths.

My priorities used to be all screwed up, in part because I thought I had to do everything myself. When I was running a multimillion dollar home improvement company, I was still cutting my own grass. I thought, "Why pay someone to do it when I can do it myself and save the money?" But I had a change of perspective when I asked a friend of mine a simple question, and it all clicked.

My pal Marc and I were visiting, and we got to discussing who we used as accountants and how much we paid for the privilege. After hearing about how great his CPA was, I asked, "Marc, how much do you pay your guy?" He told me. I nearly fainted.

"Marc, there is no way I can afford your accountant," I said, chuckling. He didn't laugh.

"Matt, the truth is you can't afford not to use my accountant."

Turns out, he was right. That very skilled, very expensive CPA saved me a lot of money. He was worth his fee because quality costs money, and he knew what he was worth.

So this experience hit me as I was riding the lawn mower one afternoon. I grabbed my iPhone from my pocket and opened up the calculator. I typed in my yearly income, then divided it by the number of daylight hours in a year and came out with $300/hour. When I worked on my business, or consulted, or set up new projects, my earning potential averaged 300 bucks – and it turns out that guys don't charge 300 bucks an hour to cut your lawn once a week.

I hired a landscaper.

It's amazing how one lesson leads to another. Prioritizing taught me how to leverage the power of personnel in both my corporate life and personal life.

See, making money is great. But it's really just a tool for getting other things that we want. We make money to give us freedom, to give us time, which is God's most precious gift. I once saw someone write the word out like this:

T - Today
I - Is
M - My
E - Everything

We get things jumbled up a lot of the time. We try to sideline our families or our passions or our spiritual lives so that we can focus on making money. But the real currency is time, and when you look at your list of priorities, you need to look at how you're spending your time. And that should light a fire under your ass to be willing to say no, to kick the time-suckers out of your life, and to find the whos to help you with your hows. That way, you create more money, more freedom, and you live a life you would actually want.

Nowadays, I guard time with God jealously. I make time to spend with my wife. We even share a calendar now, that syncs on both our phones. That way we're aware of what the other is up to and we can be on the same page. It's great – except when I show up to her doctor's appointments from time to time. Turns out, a man doesn't typically set a lot of OB-GYN appointments, and I need to increase the font size on my phone.

But you get the picture.

Some people out there will say, "Listen, Matt, that's all well and good for you. You've made your money, you've spent your sweat, and the hustle got you to where you are today. Now, from your privilege, you're trying to tell me, a single mother, or a 22-year-old man, or a busy college student, etc. that I need to say no to more and somehow my rent will get paid?"

It's a great question. But being as how I've been a young guy hustling to prove myself, get ahead, and provide for my family, I can say that I could have done it all differently and achieved results that were at least as good – and probably better. I don't have a forty-hour a week job now, sure, and that's helpful in crafting my schedule, but I do have more responsibilities than ever. The principle outlined in this chapter makes it possible for me to accomplish what all I need to do and still feel like life isn't on fast-forward.

So here's where I'll leave you to your thoughts. Maybe take a few minutes before you read the next principle and slow down to think. I'm not going to pretend that I can tell you what your priorities should be. But I'd be willing to bet that you have a good idea of what is and is not most important to you.

Make a list. Ask yourself if your priorities match with reality. If not, you've got to take an audit of your life and look hard at where your time and money are going. Maybe you're trying to do it all on your own, but you don't know the kind of person who can help you get things in balance. Find them. Network. Find a tribe (Principle #6).

Because it's the true cost of things we need to look at. Cutting my own lawn didn't save me $400 a month like I thought. It was costing me $2,400 a month in lost potential earnings. And that's just the money – it cost me several hours that could have been spent on work I was passionate about, or time with my family.

I've told you my priorities. What are yours?

PRINCIPLE
3

CALL YOUR SHOTS

OR

Dream It and Do It; VISION; Laser Focus;
X Marks the Spot; In It to Win It;
Program Your Mind

The year was 1932. America was in the midst of the Great Depression, and sports provided an escape from the difficulties of everyday life. Sure, some people were football fans, and a good many people liked boxing. But everyone was a baseball fan. People were crazy for it.

It was October 1st, and the New York Yankees and the Chicago Cubs were tied 4-4 in the fifth inning of the third game of the World Series in Chicago. The Yankees had an impressive roster, with the likes of Lou Gherig, Tony Lazzeri, and Earle Combs. But the heart and soul of the team was the legendary Babe Ruth.

Ruth was in his 18th year in the league, playing the last World Series of his career, and he was amazing – but at 37 years old, his body was showing signs of age. He wasn't as thin as he had once been, and his run was slow and kind of awkward, but he could still hit the ball with the best of them.

But hitting in baseball isn't a walk in the park. The greatest men to play the game got on base in only around 30% of their at-bats. So when George Herman "Babe" Ruth took the plate, looking for a way to break the Cubs' defense, success was not guaranteed.

The weight of the series rested on his shoulders – a living legend in hostile territory during an ugly game. The crowd yelled so loud that you couldn't hear yourself think, much less speak. The dugouts hollered at one another constantly, mocking and threatening one another. But when Charlie Root threw the first pitch of Babe's at-bat, you couldn't help but hold your breath.

It was outside, and Ruth didn't swing, but the ump called it a strike. Babe looked at the umpire, annoyed, tried to ignore the crowd's jeering, and lined up again with his bat ready.

The pitcher threw a hot one, and Ruth stepped towards it but stopped before he swung. It might have been a ball, but the ump said Ruth had crowded the batter's box, and he called that a strike. The announcer didn't like the call, but the game went on, and the other team's players were letting Ruth have it. The Cubs threw insults; the fans threw trash.

But then Babe Ruth did something that the world will always remember. He took a step back, looked at the Cub's bench, and pointed past centerfield. He was saying that he'd send the next one over the pitcher's head, over the fence, and past the flagpole.

He was not only saying that he'd hit a home run on the next pitch; he was saying where he'd hit it – out of the park in the most difficult direction. He was calling his shot.

Root wound up, delivered the pitch, and you know what the Babe did. He cracked that ball up the center line, past the pitcher, over the fence, and past the flagpole. He hit the ball nearly 500 feet, pushing the Yankees to a 6-4 lead and an eventual sweep of the World Series.

The greatest player in the history of baseball pulled it off. But before he did it, he saw it happen.

That's the power of vision.

There's a scripture that says the people perish for lack of vision. When someone is very successful and innovative we call them a visionary. "Vision" itself is a simple word that literally just means to see. But if you ask the average person about what their vision for their life is... well, you usually don't get a satisfactory answer.

And this can go wrong in two ways.

1. The person's vision is just fantasy, untethered from their life. They have no real intention of working towards fulfilling it.
2. They don't have vision at all, and like a car driving in fog, they are crawling along at 3 miles per hour, hoping that they don't drive off a cliff. They can't see past their immediate problems and concerns.

Everyone should have a vision for their life, and the truth is, beginning that process isn't even very hard. For our purposes here, vision is just the imagination it takes to see what you'll look like and what you'll be doing in 5, 10, or 20 years in the future. Remember the McConoughey speech from Principle #1? Who exactly is the future you that you're chasing?

This isn't complicated, but that doesn't mean it isn't tricky. For 'problem #1' people, when they sit down to cast a vision for their life, they go for glitzy images of fame, excess, and leisure – not necessarily because they're passionate about those things or that those are real core desires, but because our culture tells them to desire those things. This person isn't connecting with their genuine self, and is letting someone else do the vision-casting for them. That's not going to be successful.

For one kind of person, we've got to remember to reach upward, but to also know what time of day it is and be in touch with reality. Despite what Ms. Donahue, your beloved second grade teacher told you, any one of you cannot really grow up to be president. If you're 5 foot nothing, you aren't going to be a professional basketball player. But deep down, how many people really want to be president or a professional basketball player anyway? Often, these things are just manifestations of our desire for attention, freedom from financial hardship, and hoping we won't have to work too hard. Where is your potential? What does it seem like you might have been made to do? Why did God put you on this earth, and what gets you really excited? Start there. What does the best version of you look like 5 years from now?

For the other kind of person, 'problem #2' people, they've got the Eyore issue: always depressed, always putting the blame on themselves, always expecting things to go wrong. This kind of person, when asked to vision-cast, often looks at the rent that's due next week and the appointment they have to go to later in the afternoon, and these immediate little fires take up all of their imagination. The vision they give ends up being some version of, "I'd like the road cleared for about 4 feet in front of me." This kind of person, and you know who you are, needs to dream a little bigger. Sure, you don't want to struggle with the problems right in front of you today but take a 30,000-foot view. What do you really want? How can you be a person who is really winning at the game of life? What would that person look like? What would that person's attitude be? What would that person be doing?

So if you've never walked through this before, I strongly suggest that you make yourself a cup of coffee tomorrow morning, tie on a robe, and sit on the front porch with a pad of paper and a pencil. And dream of what your life could be. What it ought to be.

Forgive me for getting theological here for a minute, but it is a central teaching of my faith that says man was created in the image of God. Now that's a deep and complex idea, but to me, that means that we've been given the ability to make choices and shape the world around us to some extent. That we were created as something good, and even though we hyper-focus on the fall from grace sometimes, we should remember that before man fell, God said he was good.

And so, we should ask ourselves how we could look in an ideal scenario. If we got our lives cleaned up and cleared the obstacles, what would we be creating? Who would we be blessing? Person #1 needs to remember that we aren't almighty God and can't just do whatever the hell we want, but person #2 needs to remember that we were made in God's image, and our potential is great.

This all culminates in a very reasonable question. If I can get that realistic, ambitious image of who I could be in 5 or 10 years into my brain, I need to start asking how that person would act in various circumstances.

This is way better than goal setting, and getting stuck in the cycle of victory, overconfidence, failure, shame, and giving up. Instead, it's the daily climb of getting into that best-version-of-you, trying on that person's boots, and asking how that person would attack what's in front of you.

If the ideal is to have six-pack abs, would you really start off every morning with a cinnamon roll and a half gallon of chocolate milk? No? Then how would this fit version of you go about getting his breakfast?

If the idea is to be making a lot of money and be out of personal debt, would you really make that impulse purchase? Would you buy as many shoes as you're tempted to buy? And for goodness' sake, would you really spend your money without a budget week after week? How would you organize your finances?

Then, with all of these things, when you decide what that ideal you would do – be a copycat and do them yourself.

How can you not end up becoming that person if you have a clear vision and constant focus on chasing that dream?

"Bobby, you're going to Ohio."

My friend Bobby looked up from what he was doing and blinked a few times.

"...What for?"

"Because I went to Ohio, and it'll blow your mind."

He looked at me, a little confused.

"Are we going on a golf trip?"

"No," I said. "I'll explain. There's a school there – a nonprofit kind of thing that educates small business owners and helps them grow their business. I learned about it from a guy in my business peer group, I went, and it helped me out a lot. Now I think you should go as well."

So that, more or less, is the first time I told someone about Aileron. I've told plenty of others, and now I'm telling all of you. I've attended their business program three times, and I recommend it highly. The main reason I get excited about it is because it is where I learned about vision.

You see, in 1970, a man named Clayton Mathile quit his job at Campbell's Soup to take a job with a start-up pet food company named Iams. At the time of his hiring, Clayton was the sixth employee at the company, and you would be excused for never having heard of them, because they were not exactly a global force in their industry.

But Clay Mathile didn't quit his steady job at a large company on a whim. He knew what he was getting into, and where he would take it. Clay had a vision, and that vision was this:

"To become the largest pet food provider in the world."

That's what he saw himself doing, and that's the level he saw himself competing at. And after twelve years of hard work and loyal service, Mathile had boosted his company to the point where they were doing $13 million in sales. Not bad for a dog food company in 1983, but it still was not what he had envisioned. He knew where he was going to end up.

So he bought the company in 1982 and ran it for 17 years, until Proctor and Gamble bought it from him in 1999 for $2.3 billion. He was the largest pet food provider in the world.

What does all of this have to do with me going to Ohio? Well, Clay decided that he was going to take some of his windfall and open a non-profit for small business owners, teaching them the management techniques that contributed to his great success. So he spent $130 million to build a campus in Dayton Ohio and called it Aileron – named after the small flaps on an aircraft's wings responsible for giving it lift. His idea was that he was going to be that little piece of the puzzle that raised up business owners around the country and got them flying.

This is where I learned about vision, from Clay and his pet food. He mentored me, and I won't ever forget the lessons that great man taught me about life and business.

I'm not an affiliate, and I don't get paid to say this, but if you ever get the chance, go to Ohio.

Anyway, after attending Aileron's program for the first time some years ago, I went home and wrote down the vision for my company, something I hadn't really done before.

I wrote, "Sell and produce $25 million annually, and remain the largest home improvement company in East Tennessee."

Suddenly, I knew what I was striving for, and when I shared it with my company, my employees knew, and my management team knew. We rallied around it. We asked ourselves how everything we did fit into that vision. I finally sat down and set the vision for my organization, and then we fulfilled it.

We did not take out a billboard on highway 24 that said, "Out here trying to sell $25 million each year and remain bigger than the other guys."

Our billboards and TV ads and print copy said, "Make it better for our customers, our coworkers, and our community." We were a home improvement company, after all, and this is a mission that everyone could get behind.

A vision is personal. A mission is public. Vision is internal. Mission is external. People mix these things up often, and that causes all kinds of confusion and wasted opportunity. If you run around telling your vision to everybody, your brain already thinks you've gotten your reward. "Good for you," people say, and it'll feel like you've already accomplished the thing. But there's nothing for people to get on board with, alongside you.

The vision is for you and your team. How we relate externally is our mission, and it's important to know what both of those things are.

Clay Mathile's vision took him years to realize, and yours might take a long time too. You may even want to tweak your vision over time, and that's ok. The point is that you've got to be working towards something. Stagnation is a failure of imagination.

There are people that have become great at attracting things in their life that they want, and they're great at getting things out of their life that they don't want. After 50 years, I've gotten pretty good at this. I'm attracted to things that bring the best out in me, not the stress out in me. I've coached people how to do this – how to get that job, that body, that relationship, those emotions. The key is to focus on that vision.

I truly believe that you were born to do something great with your life, and you were born to be happy most of the time. But what's sad is 95% of people will go through their entire life and not fulfill their dreams. They won't make the money, find the success, have the body, health, relationships, emotions or memories that they could have had. They won't feel like they did something great or had much happiness.

Why do most people go their whole life and never achieve these things? It's because they go through life reacting. You just have to have a vision of what you want and make daily strides to get closer to it.

Most of us are trying to live our lives without any real thought or planning. We're like a contractor who is trying to construct a building without a blueprint. Many of the members in one of my peer groups own "design-build" companies. I had read the term "design-build" many times in trade magazines, but I didn't truly understand its meaning until learning more about their businesses. It's simple. In a nutshell, you design something, THEN you build it. You don't start something and figure it out along the way. You define what you want before you begin. Like in construction, if we don't know the end result, we're often left out of balance and unreliable. We never fulfill the reason for our existence and end up unsatisfied and frustrated. The key to having a rewarding and productive life is developing a specific plan to fulfill your personal vision.

By way of example, I'd like to share with you my personal vision statement.

Here it is:

> I give my heart over to God. I will focus on being the best husband, father, son, and friend each day. I will repeatedly think about making things better. I know I can do something great with my life and will live my life with purpose and with the expectation that great things will come. I will look for the blessing and not the curse. I will focus on the positive, not the negative. I will choose to be around those that bring out the best in me and want to live my life without saying, "If I had only..." I will strive to get 1% better each day on my daily climb. God will lead me to do His will to connect with and help others.

I keep my personal vision written out, sitting on my computer desktop where I can see it every day. Once a year, I sit down and see if I need to revise it. That's the way life is, and we need to have some degree of flexibility. You can get this wrong by being too general with your vision or too rigid. But you can't hit the mark unless you have something to aim at.

But all of this begs the question of mindset. I'm not one of those "self-esteem leads you to success" people, and I don't do affirmations in the morning. If you do affirmations, good for you, and I'm not knocking your practice. But I suppose the point here is that even if there's no magical formula, the way you think does affect what you do.

I once heard somebody say, "Whether you think you can do it or not, you're right." That's the power of a self-fulfilling prophecy. A great vision and a terrible mindset is an incomplete equation. So it's worth taking a moment to examine your mindset – especially if you're having trouble with casting a vision in the first place.

What is "mindset"? It's a word we use a lot, but what does it mean to you?

Webster says it is "a mental attitude or inclination." And as more than one smart person has pointed out over the years, attitude is everything.

The way I see it, there are essentially two mindsets:

A fixed mindset sees the way life is right now as the way it's always going to be. The trajectory will never change. What you see is what you get.

A growth mindset knows that change and improvement are possible. Things could be different tomorrow, and you'll have to adapt. What you see could change, with time, effort, or luck of the draw.

A fixed mindset is not usually looking for opportunities, and if it does look, it's only looking in one narrow lane of things that have worked before.

A growth mindset keeps a broader vision, looking for whatever is helpful to your growth and goals.

A fixed mindset hunkers down and deals with it when there's a problem.

A growth mindset asks how we can eliminate the problem.

A fixed mindset says the pie is only so big and can only feed so many people.

A growth mindset says, "How can we get a bigger pie?"

I want you to know, as I've learned throughout the course of my life, that you have the opportunity to be happier and more effective because of your mindset.

For my purposes, I think of five attributes to the right kind of growth mindset:

1. Intentional
2. Prioritized
3. Positive (A Good Attitude)
4. Open to Good Things Coming
5. All While Having a Good Time (or, Joyful, if you want it in one word)

If your mindset is not intentional, you'll be unfocused. Another term for that is "double-minded," and you can't make any progress when you're constantly pulling the steering wheel left, then right, and back and forth. The car doesn't function well with your feet on the gas and the brakes at the same time.

I had a cousin many years ago that was overserved at a bar. He made the right decision to not drive and called me to come pick him up. I said, "Where are you?" He said, "I'm next to this bar at an Amoco gas station. When you're coming down the road, it will either be on your left or your right." In his drunken state, he actually made an accurate statement, but the point is you can't be both.

If you aren't prioritized, your efforts will not lead you where you want to go, leaving you out of place. If you don't know what you should be doing, someone will tell you. But their idea of what you should be doing is sure to be different than yours.

If you don't have a good attitude, then you'll have a bad one. Bitterness is no way to live, let me tell you. The right mindset is pragmatic and optimistic, so it is always hopeful, but it can roll with the punches when setbacks come. Use the difficulty.

If you are not open to good things coming your way, you'll often miss them when they do.

And if you don't keep your joy and wonder, if you can't have a good time doing it, you'll quit. At some point, you can't function without any enthusiasm whatsoever. Without gratitude, why bother? There are some spiritual things that we just can't live without past a certain point, and if you can't sing on your way into battle, you won't be fighting for very long.

To sum that up, the wrong kind of mindset for us Daily Climbers is the mirror image of the one I laid out on the previous page. If you aren't setting your mind rightly, you will be:

1. Ineffective
2. Lost
3. Negative
4. Missing Out
5. Burned Out

I don't know about you, but I like that first list a whole lot better than the second.

Life does have its challenges. I heard a Vietnam veteran speaking many years ago, and he talked about his time in the "Hanoi Hotel," a prison camp for captured Americans where there was a lot of torture. To paraphrase what he said: "It was surprising to see who broke and who didn't. The pessimists broke first. They were ready for things to go south, and when they did, they were quick to throw their hands up. No surprise there. But after them came the optimists. The ones who said,

'We'll be out by Easter,' did really well in the prison camp – until Easter came, and we weren't out. Then they'd go into a dark depression. But they'd rally once or twice and say, 'We'll be out by Christmas, for sure.' But then Christmas would come and they weren't rescued, and they'd break."

"So who didn't break?" someone asked.

"The hopeful realists," he quickly replied. "The ones who said, 'This is going to be hard on me, but there's a chance I'll make it. But even if I don't, someone is going to make it, and my goal will be accomplished in end, whether it's by me or by someone else."

You and I haven't been to any prison camps, most likely, and thankfully, most of the time we don't have to think in terms of "If I die, someone else will carry it on." But we do all have hardships, and we can learn from that soldier's story.

The world's going to throw some curveballs at you. When it rains, it pours, and sometimes a sunny day gets rained out too. So this requires a habitual practice of picking yourself up off the ground and setting your mind where it needs to be.

I'll be vulnerable with you for a minute here to make a point. I don't feel sorry for myself, and I don't want you to either, but I have arthritis and joint pain that's pretty severe, and it's been that way for a couple of decades now. Sometimes it is hard to even get out of bed in the morning, but I get out of bed anyway. Once I'm up and I get going, it's ok. Things get a little better. At the end of the day, I don't have to say, "Gee, I wish I'd accomplished something today." Sometimes you're hurting and you don't have all of your ducks in a row, but to start, you only need one duck, as somebody once said. Getting going can be the majority of the battle, and you can improve your efforts if only you first have the courage to start.

So I set my mind every day. I read over my vision for my personal life and for my businesses. Writing this book is a discipline I've chosen to help set my mind. And every day when I wake up, I send an email to my online subscribers, giving them a little bit of encouragement and something to chew on. I get as much out of it as they do.

Keep in mind that maintaining a growth mindset takes some discipline, and discipline requires disciplines – specific practices that shape you in a particular way. I don't know what your aspirations are. I don't know the person you hope to be. But once you do, you may find it helpful to look for a few disciplines that you can take part in regularly to keep you on course.

Stumbling is ok. Trial and error is part of the process. You won't get it right on the first try, but you are likely to get better the longer you keep at it. We don't want to be like the kid who asks, "Why do I have to bathe? I'm going to just get dirty again."

We want to be the kind of people who get clean and don't spend all of their time filthy, right?

The tide pushes backwards, so learn to swim. And if you're going to swim, you may as well do it with a smile on your face.

Clarity (vision) + intentionality (mindset) = the freedom to have your priorities straight.

So who do you want to be?

PRINCIPLE
4

WHAT GOES AROUND COMES AROUND

OR

Don't Spit in the Wind; Karma; To Whom Much Is Given, Much Is Required; Be Open to the Unexpected; Lend a Hand

The following is a story that was published about 20 years ago, in a book called <u>Chicken Soup for the Soul</u>. I'd like to share it with you now:

> Mark was walking home from school one day when he noticed the boy ahead of him had tripped and dropped all of the books he was carrying, along with two sweaters, a baseball bat, a glove, and a small tape recorder. Mark knelt down and helped the boy pick up the scattered articles. Since they were going the same way, he helped to carry the burden.

As they walked, Mark discovered the boy's name was Bill, that he loved video games, baseball, and history, that he was having a lot of trouble with his other subjects and that he had just broken up with his girlfriend. They arrived at Bill's home first, and Mark was invited in for a Coke and to watch some T.V. The afternoon passed pleasantly with a few laughs and some shared small talk, then Mark went home.

They continued to see each other around school, had lunch together once or twice. They ended up at the same high school where they had brief contacts over the years. Finally, the long awaited senior year came, and three weeks before graduation, Bill asked Mark if they could talk. Bill reminded him of the day years ago when they had first met.

"Do you ever wonder why I was carrying so many things from school that day?" asked Bill. "You see, I cleaned out my locker because I didn't want to leave a mess for anyone else. I had stored away some of my mother's pills and I was going home to commit suicide. But after we spent some time together I realized that if I had, I would have missed that time and so many others that might follow. So you see, Mark, when you picked up my books for me that day, you did a lot more. You saved my life."

This story may sound like a parable, or an urban legend, and I don't blame you for being skeptical. But this happened. The man who wrote the story was a teacher at the boys' junior high school, and he says that they grew closer over the years, and Bill and Mark ended up being each other's best man at their respective weddings. One is now a minister, and the other a successful business man.

So what is the point of this story? Why do I mention it here?

Because you can miss a field goal by kicking too far left, too far right, or by not kicking the ball hard enough to be begin with. We need balance in our approach to life if we want to hit the mark, because there are a lot of ways we can get it wrong or miss out.

So, after all of this talk in the previous principles about having your priorities set, getting the right mindset, and not letting negative or toxic people bring you down, we need to balance that truth with the need for openness. We don't always know what God is going to send our way in a given day. Hell, we just about never know, and if we're too rigid in our plans, we'll miss the chance to be part of something extraordinary.

Squire Rushnell calls this sort of a thing a "Godwink." Webster's dictionary calls it serendipity. As for me, I just say what goes around comes around. And it's worth slowing down from time to time, being aware of others around you who may need a hand up, and sometimes being the one to give it to them.

I imagine that boy Mark from the story had other plans that day he saw Bill tripping over his books. Maybe he could have been seen as a nerd for helping someone with such an apparent desire to study. But he was not so focused on himself that he would miss the opportunity to do a little good in the world.

Jenny and I have our own family foundation, and one of the non-profits we support is The Jason Foundation. They raise awareness and prevention for teenage suicide. They operate in all 50 states and had saved hundreds, if not thousands, of lives. A man named Clark Flatt started the foundation after his son Jason took his own life at 16 years old.

My daughter's high school has chapel one day per week, and they invite speakers to talk with the entire student body. I asked Clark to come speak one time, and I'm very glad that I did. Clark talked about the warning signs, what to look for, how to be a friend, and about the day Jason committed suicide. That morning, Jason called 2 of his friends and told them when, how, and where he'd take his life. Clark doesn't blame them now. They were kids; they didn't know what to do. One said he thought he'd get in trouble. Clark told the students if they felt any desire to ever take their life to please talk to someone: a friend, a preacher, a teacher or parent. Later that evening, Reverend Gallimore reached out to me. A 14-year-old female student came to his office that afternoon and asked for help.

Saving a life is worth more than all of the accomplishments, financial rewards, and progress in the world, isn't it? Or even just helping someone find the tools they need to get out of a dark time in their life.

Since I've learned to start living this way – being open to what the day might bring me – I've made a lot of friends, helped a lot of people, and maybe, just maybe started on the track of leaving this world a little bit better than I found it.

I recently had an entire week where every day was scheduled with a lunch to give someone a dose of much-needed advice. They'd reached out to see if I could lend a hand.

As you may already be aware, I'm strict with my schedule. I have no problems with cancelling an engagement if I think it doesn't suit my purposes, and I've cut people out of my regular social circle if they aren't living in a positive direction. But when someone is in need of some advice or help, and I can supply it to them, I see that as a different kind of opportunity.

At the end of that week, my wife Jenny said, "Matt, you give and you give, and you don't get anything in return."

As is often the case in marriage, I didn't have any idea what she was talking about. So I asked her.

"You're burdening yourself with all these people's problems," she said, talking about the lunch appointments. "These people all got thousands of dollars in free consulting, but you're sort of left holding the bag, without getting something for it." She was genuinely concerned about my stress and workload.

I said, "I did get something for it. It's not as tangible as a consulting check or equity in a company, but I get peace and joy from helping somebody out, and that ultimately makes me happier." What goes around comes around.

I'm a competitive guy. I know that. And I don't think I'll ever quit business entirely, or be uninterested when I have an opportunity to build a great company or make some money. But I think that helping each other and having openness to life is how God designed us to live. It's honestly changed my life. It's made me less selfish. It's kept me from growing hardened to the world.

Ironically, when I look back on the meetings I've taken with no upside, the people I've assisted who can't repay me, and the introductions I've made on behalf of others' interests – I do get something out of it. I'm known as a connector now. My network keeps growing and growing. And even though we don't do this sort of thing for getting something out of it, I'd like to share a few stories with you of how living with open hands has filled them up in ways I never imagined.

I've had countless occasions where this sort of thing came together to make some big changes in my life. Here are a couple.

The first was when my friend Phillip Fulmer invited me to fly on the team plane to watch the Tennessee men's basketball squad play in an early season game against #1 ranked Gonzaga in 2018. He's a nation-championship-winning college football coach, and by this time he was the athletic director, so he has those kind of connections. The game was all the way in Phoenix, but it sounded like a lot of fun, so I was up for it. On the day of the flight, however, Coach Fulmer was unable to go. He encouraged me to go anyway.

I was hesitant. I didn't know anyone. I didn't want to be the random stowaway on the team airplane.

"Who are you?"

"Me? Oh, I know the athletic director. He invited me. Even though he isn't coming. Really."

Yeah. Running that scenario through in my head was awkward.

But, what the heck? Phillip assured me it would be fine, and said that he had a friend named Rick in Arizona who would show me around and host. So that's how I met Rick Federico. We got into town 2 days before the game, giving us time to play golf at Whisper Rock and strike up as fast friends. Rick, as it turned out, was the chairman of the board at PF Chang's. He's a rock star in the restaurant industry. A fun weekend turned into a lasting friendship, and Rick and I go fly fishing once in a while, we golf, go to UT games, and our families spend time together.

Not long after Rick retired from his chairmanship, he called me up.

"Matt," he said. "Turns out retirement doesn't suit me. I'm bored. Why don't you join me and let's open up a new restaurant?"

When someone like Rick asks you to open a restaurant with him, it's a no-brainer. We now own Thompson 105 in Scottsdale, Arizona, and it's been a blast.

Rick Federico ended up introducing me to another Rick, who I never would have known otherwise. Rick Grayson was the founder and owner of a coffee company called "Cult." And, no, he wasn't in a cult. Just an edgy name for his regionally successful roastery.

Grayson and I got to talking about his operation easily. He'd been in the game for a long time and had a great product, but he needed the sort of level-up management strategy that I'd learned in my peer groups over the years, at Aileron business school, and in growing my home improvement business. And having sold my company, I was looking for something to do.

Rick and I kept sort of looking at one another throughout the conversation, thinking, "Business opportunities can't be this easy, can they?"

We ended up going into business together. Go figure. I'm glad I got on that plane in 2018.

A few years later, I found myself at the Four Seasons Hotel, once again in Scottsdale Arizona. I was attending a private equity annual investor conference, and on the last night the company hosted a singer-songwriter concert.

This wasn't your typical, high-rise hotel, keep in mind. Our rooms were in "casitas," scattered over a large, beautiful property. It was a lot of fun, but it did mean you had to do some walking.

Well, on the night of the concert, I was halfway along the long, winding path that led to the lobby, when I realized something completely unimportant:

I'd forgotten my belt.

A crime of fashion, maybe, but my blazer covered it up anyhow, and the pants fit fairly well. I started forward again, breathing in the night air and looking around at the cacti.

I stopped again. Call it ADD, OCD, or set in my ways, but damn it, I wasn't the sort of guy to show up without a belt when I had intended to wear one.

Whatever.

So, I turned a one-eighty and headed back to my room. There was the belt. Sitting on my bed like it had been waiting for me. I threw it on and headed back out the door, hoping I wouldn't be late and miss the first song.

The reason why all these details matter is that when I got back out to the winding pathway and started along it again, another gentlemen came out of his casita and walked alongside me. He said, "Hi. My name is Tim."

Friendly guy. I introduced myself and asked what he did. I told him I was there for the private equity event, and turns out he was too. I told him I was an investor in a coffee company there that I'd visited earlier that day on our free time break. He said, "My neighbor just sold his coffee company for 'a large number,'" and then he stopped right there and sent a group text to me and his neighbor Chad. (As a result, Chad and I had a conference call the next week, and now we are working together.)

We continued to walk toward the concert venue, and Tim suddenly went deep.

"Matt, what's your purpose?"

"You know Tim," I replied. "I've been trying to figure that out. I love my family. I like helping people. I love business, but I don't know if I can say exactly. What's yours?"

"I had a healthy exit from the healthcare industry," he said, "and now my sole purpose is to tell people about Jesus."

I don't know how that comes across on paper, but in person, it was clear that I was talking to a genuine guy. No fake stuff. He wasn't trying to preach. He wasn't selling long-distance plans, essential oils, or an exciting new opportunity.

He really was solely there to tell people about Jesus, and to offer them help, if he could. No ax to grind. No other agenda. Just an adventurer taking life one day at a time, grateful to be there and looking to do some good.

We arrived at the concert to a lady holding a tray of cabernet, so Tim and I had a glass of wine together, then headed to our tables for the concert, but not before he introduced me to an entertainment lawyer named Derek who was well connected in the country music industry. Fascinating guy, and we didn't know what we had in common exactly, but we made conversation and learned about each other's work, and we hit it off as friends.

The mingling died down once the music started, and it was easy to see why. Songwriters Hunter Phelps, Chris DeStefano, and Ashley Gorley performed. It was amazing. Ashley Gorley alone has 65 number one songs under his belt – more than any other songwriter from any genre of music ever. It was quite special.

During the show, I looked around for Tim. He was 2 tables away, and each time I looked in his direction, he was leaning over to the woman next to him in deep conversation. I thought to myself, "Why are they not paying attention to this incredible concert?"

At the conclusion of the show, the hosts said they were moving the bar outside and serving s'mores. I found Tim.

"What were you and that lady talking about, Tim? Is that your wife? Girlfriend?"

"No," he said. "Matt, I just met her. I told her what my purpose was. She ended up asking questions, told me she was an atheist, and by the end of the concert she agreed to call me tomorrow."

"Why is she calling you tomorrow?"
He shrugged, like it was obvious.

"So I can pray with her."

She did call him the next day. And the next, and the next. She ended up calling him every day for thirty days, so he could tell her about Jesus and pray for her.

Tim is living out his purpose.

By the time they shut the bar down the night of the concert, 5 of us held hands while Tim prayed for us. Tim and I now counsel each other, and he's became a great friend.

Fast-forward a few months, and all this comes together. Derek and another friend named Jeff proposed that I take a large equity stake and run a new e-commerce business as its CEO to take the brand nationwide. We'll use influencers to promote coffee, apparel, and whiskey, adding additional products along the way. Derek represents a lot of country music's biggest stars, so he set me up with a tour through Nashville, meeting famous musicians and getting co-promotion agreements with them. I got hooked up with people at a couple of major league sports teams, and we're looking into more partnership deals. The company is going to be a "Tom's Shoes" sort of thing where every time someone buys our coffee, we donate to charity. Specifically, a portion of each sale goes to The Jason Foundation to help raise awareness and to prevent teenage suicide.

We're calling it "Nashville Grind."

When I look back on this series of unlikely events, I've gotten to meet all of these incredible performers, hobnob in the music and sports world, expand my network, and I've not only gotten a job I'm passionate about – I've gotten some good friends out of it too.

All because I forgot my belt and got on an airplane.

Everything happens for a reason, they say. But the trick is to live like you believe that. Because at the end of the day, it's not our plan; it's God's plan.

You just never know who you're going to meet.

In 2016, I drove to Amelia Island for a roofing conference. I arrived at the hotel around dinnertime, so I checked into my room, threw my bags down, and headed to the poolside restaurant. It had been a long drive, and I was starving and really thirsty, so I just sat at the bar. I needed to call home and touch base with Jenny, but realized I hadn't charged my phone. I was on 1% battery.

Just then, a man and his wife sat down next to me. He had one of those battery packs on the back of his phone. (I think they were called Mophies?)

"Excuse me," I said to the man, "but if you'll give me some juice for my phone, I'll buy y'all's first drink."

He took that deal, and now years later, Keith Byrd is one of my best friends. We even have second homes next to one another. Strangely enough, Keith's book, From the Broom Closet to Park Avenue is being released the same year as this book.

I never would have met him if I'd been afraid of talking to strangers – or if my phone had been charged.

———

"For everyone to whom much is given, from him much will be required."

Those are 13 words from Jesus that I can never get out of my head.

I'm at a point in my life where there is no denying that much has been given to me. And I'll be honest, I like "being given." So do you, I'd bet. I've been blessed with a beautiful wife, a wonderful daughter, great parents, the best of friends, a comfortable home, vacations, and cool belongings. But I recognize the second part of that verse as well – "much will be required."

I'm not afraid to discuss my faith around others, but I do it in a tactful way. I know I'm a sinner, and I may be on my second bourbon when I bring it up, but I do. Even around people I've not met, I always begin dinner with prayer and say, "It's a Southern thing, but we hold hands when we pray if y'all don't mind." If the waiter or waitress walks up, I often say, "We're about to pray. Is there anything we can pray for you for?" Last week a young lady joined in our hand holding, and we prayed for her upcoming college exam.

I met one of my business partners in a restaurant parking lot about a month ago, and he handed me a distribution check from our company. It was a good check, and I worked hard for it. I was happy to get it. But I found even more joy in giving part of it to my friend Brian, whose son is suffering from a rare form of MS. Brian needed a break – and a friend. Anyone who's been in a medical crisis knows about that. Helping Brian out meant more to me than just adding a few digits to my bank account, or taking another vacation, or buying into another business.

He's a child of God just like the rest of us, isn't he? So was that waitress we prayed with at the restaurant. I think God expects those who are able, to help.

I don't think I'm the only one He expects this of, however. You don't have to be financially well off in order to have been given "much."

Some people have a lot of friends, and sitting next to the loner in the company break room can do a lot of good.

Some people have a lot of free time, and they can put it to use fixing a single mother's broken refrigerator, or covering a shift for a friend in a tight spot.

Some people have a lot of creativity and encouragement, and they can use those gifts to lift people up.

Some people don't have a lot of money, but they're generous with it anyway. Jesus said something about that, too. The widow and her two pennies, if you're familiar with the story.

I guess the principle is, when you're driving by a homeless person who looks like they're really trying – or really in a bad spot – and you think, "Lord, send somebody to help that poor soul." Maybe have a little bit of self-awareness and realize that you could be the solution.

We all need to learn to wake up with the realization that today, we could be the answer to somebody's prayer. Be a difference maker.

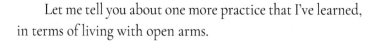

Let me tell you about one more practice that I've learned, in terms of living with open arms.

It's called "insist."

If someone gives you "insist," that means that no matter what they ask of you, no matter when, and no matter how expensive or inconvenient it will be, you do what that person asks.

It's a risk to give "insist" to anyone, and quite a treasure to have it. Naturally you want to be careful who you give it to.

As with all of the good things in my life, I was first shown this idea by another, wiser person, and I took notes.

A lot of my friends tend to be older than I am. My wife says it's because I have an old soul, and maybe that's true. One such friend was a man who was close with my father, named Jim Monroe, and I met him in Orlando, Florida at the 1994 Fiesta Bowl. I was twenty years old, Tennessee was playing Penn State, my dad and mom had sprung for a nice hotel room for my sister and me, next to theirs, next to Jim's room that he shared with his wife. Unbeknownst to my father, when I met Jim he offered to make me a cocktail. As someone still a year away from being a legal drinker, this intrigued me. So I made a mental note to meet up with Jim later.

We went to the football game, and it was an emotional rollercoaster. Tennessee was up 10-0 at the half, and we were ready to roll them. Penn State's coach, Joe Paterno, paced the sidelines with his arms crossed, studying us, trying to figure out what to do, but we were unbeatable. Well, until they came out roaring in the second half and beat us like a drum. Tennessee lost 13-31.

I snuck out of my room that night and found Jim to take him up on his offer. He made me a drink, and despite not quite being 21 yet, I was not struck by lightning, so I decided to enjoy myself. I sat up half the night drinking with Jim and talking about everything under the sun. We developed a great friendship.

Shortly after that trip, Jim called me up and asked me to come to his house, because he had something to give me. When I arrived, I was surprised to find that he had nothing in his hands. He wasn't standing next to an obvious gift, and he didn't tell me to follow him into the other room, where the thing he wanted to give me was.

He just said, "Matt, your dad and I are great friends, and you and I have become friends too. I want to give you 'insist.'"

I said, "Huh?"

He laughed, in a good-natured kind of way.

"If you're ever in trouble," he explained, "if you're in a ditch, down and out, or in jail, you just call and say, 'I insist.' You must treat 'insist' very seriously, but all you have to do is call and say those two words, and I'll be there for you no matter what."

I never used it, but I kept it close to my heart, and I've given 'insist' to many of my friends over the years. My friend Kraig Mackett, who is like a brother to me, says he still remembers fondly the day I gave it to him.

None of us have ever used it, but it's peaceful to know that it's there. You rest a little easier knowing that your friends are there for you, and you ought to be there for them as well.

So, ask yourself: Do you have anyone who would run to your rescue should the occasion call for it? Do you have friends who would drop everything they're doing, jump on a plane on a moment's notice, and fly to your rescue? If you don't, I suggest you deepen a few of the relationships around you.

And if you do have those people in your life, I suggest you send them a message today. Tell them thanks for being the kind of friend that will be there for you in time of need.

Ask yourself another question: Do you belong to a like-minded community that shares your values, your philosophy, and your commitments? Shoot, I want all my relationships to be this way.

The point is this – somewhere along the line, you've got to ask yourself if you're so hyper focused on your own goals and visions that you forget about the people around you.

I heard a story about a tech billionaire, who supposedly spent his last words screaming at a nurse for bringing him the wrong kind of juice. There's something tragic about that. He forgot about those around him.

Or are you so focused on your plan that you miss excellent opportunities to innovate?

In 2013, Jamie Siminoff brought his "ring video doorbell" system to Shark Tank, looking for a partner. All five of the sharks turned him down. Five years later, he sold his company to Amazon for $1 billion.

Are you so keyed into your own needs, that you've forgotten the joy of meeting a need for someone else – even someone who doesn't deserve it?

I'll let you answer that last question without an example from me to cloud your mind. Relationships are what endure when everything else fades away. And if you've ever been in need, or down and out, or depressed, or in need of a break, when someone reached down to give you a hand, then you know the sort of magic even a small gesture of kindness can create.

I know I do.

I'll give you one more bit of Bible:

"Remember the words of the Lord Jesus, that He said, 'It is more blessed to give than to receive.'"

Have you ever seen a shooting star or witnessed something amazing that you wish you could go back 2 minutes, run inside to get your family, and watch it again? Those moments come and go quick, but they aren't accidental. Nothing is accidental. Yes, what goes around comes around, but it's not by chance. God is moving and working all around us, all the time. But more often than not, we've got our head stuck in our phone, too busy and fixed on getting through the day. We're not looking past the immediate present, not looking for what God's doing all around us. We're just looking at our watch, thinking of where we need to be next, our to-do list, and wondering how to get everything done.

But if you fix your heart and your mindset to recognize the presence of God, who he places in front of you, where he directs you and be open to that path, then you will see His fingerprints are everywhere you go.

Psalm 130:6 says, "My soul waits for the Lord more than watchmen for the morning; indeed, more than the watchmen for the morning."

It's the watching, the moment of quiet, and recognizing that God is involved in what happens.

This principle is longer than then the others, as it's the heart and soul of the book. You see, when Jesus said, "To whom much is given, much is required," to me that means give and receive.

If we are blessed with talents, wealth, knowledge, time, and the like, it is expected that we use these well to glorify God and benefit others.

When you have intention but do not follow through, you don't give anything. When you have intention but no direction, you don't accomplish anything. Intention doesn't mean shit, really.

My friend George says a person like this is "all hat and no cattle," a wannabe, a talker, a waste.

What's required is for you to take action. Put your money where your mouth is. Reflect back on Principle #3 where we discuss mindset.

1 John 3:18 says, "My children [that's us], let us not love in word or speech, but in action and truth."

There it is: action. Even taking the "action" to be aware of your surroundings is action.

Jesus also says in the book of Luke, "Do not judge and you won't be judged," "Do not condemn and you will not be condemned," and "Forgive, and you will be forgiven."

Sounds like "what goes around comes around," doesn't it?

PRINCIPLE
5

FIND A GUIDE

OR

*Never Fly Fish Alone; Learn from the
Master; Don't Reinvent the Wheel;
Humble Thyself; Study First; Stand on
the Shoulders of Giants*

I hope heaven is similar to Enchanted Lake Lodge in
Katamai, National Park, Alaska.

Spanning 4.2 million acres, Katamai is a never-ending
view. As the plane dips below the clouds and the land opens
up before you, you can see shimmering blue-green glaciers,
steaming volcanoes, and waterfalls everywhere. It's home
to moose, wolves, caribou, and more bald eagles than you
can imagine.

Enchanted Lake Lodge is perched just above the crystal-clear Nonvianuk Lake in Katamai. It's one of the most beautiful places I've ever been, and I go back every year with a group of 12 friends.

Because, in addition to being an absolutely gorgeous place to be, Katamai National Park is home to some of the best trout fishing on the planet.

A man named Darren Erickson and his wife Tracy run the lodge where we stay, and when I say they "run" it, I mean it wouldn't operate without them. Daren makes sure that the float planes are in tiptop shape, that the fishing rods and reels are perfect, that the supplies are plentiful, the propane tanks are full, and that the food and wine are top-shelf. The employees, the rooms, the experience – everything about this place is just first class. I'd say it's my little secret except that I'm writing about it here, in this book.

On top of all I've told you about Darren, he also knows just where to fish. He knows how to handle the bears when they come around. He knows how heavy your rod ought to be, what streamer to tie on, and which way to cast.

My point is, Enchanted Lake Lodge doesn't work without Darren. He and Tracy are the "Who" that you need to make it all work up there, and Darren is a damn good friend and one heck of a guide.

And so let me tell you what I've learned in these annual fishing trips, and others:

Don't go fishing without a guide.

I've learned a lot in my years of fly-fishing, but the above sentence is my biggest takeaway.

But why should that be? I've got plenty of experience, and I'm no dummy. I've landed prize fish from Alaska all the way to the Bahamas, but whenever I'm going to fish somewhere new, the first thing I do is make sure to hire a local guide.

There are thousands of kinds of fish, and you know what's funny? They don't like to eat the same things. And take one particular fish – say a Rainbow Trout, for example. They don't eat the same kind of thing throughout the year. It shifts depending on when certain kinds of bugs are hatching, or molting, or whatever it might be.

So if you're tying on a fly to lure a rainbow trout, you need to know what they're going to be in the mood for. If it's, say, March or April, they'll probably want a mayfly. But just a month or so later, they'll be wanting to munch on a caddisfly. Midsummer? They'll be on the hunt for stonefly. And these kinds of lures do not look similar. The fish know the difference.

This is all without even mentioning tide patterns, underwater structure preferences, water depth (which depends on the season), wind, phases of the moon, feeding times, or breeding grounds.

If you toss a line in the water at random, you might catch a good time, but usually that'll be it. Steven Wright put it best when he said:

"There's a fine line between fishing and standing on the shore looking like an idiot."

Norman Maclean wrote maybe the best depiction of fly fishing ever in his classic, A River Runs Through It. Even if you are not a fisherman, you may have heard of this because of the movie they made from it, starring Brad Pitt with Robert Redford directing.

The story takes place in Montana, one of the best fly fishing spots in the world, and two brothers, Norman and Paul get together to catch some trout. Norman loves to fish, and he's skilled at it. But his brother Paul is an anomaly. Fly fishing is his passion. From childhood, it's all he's ever really cared about. He knows how the fish tick, every detail, where they swim, and what they want.

Rain or shine, good days and bad days, Paul's creel comes home loaded with fish. The best strategy for Norm is to watch Paul, pick his brain, and copy what he does.

This has been my experience as well. When you want to catch some fish, let the guide show you where to go.

As a wise teacher once hollered out to some fishermen in the Sea of Galilee, "Throw the net in on the *other side* of the boat!"

And those fishermen must have felt stupid, because damn if it didn't work. Zero fish on the left side, but the net bursts from all the fish on the right side. The world is like that sometimes.

I myself have had a number of guides throughout my life. Some have been pivotal to my success and education for a short season, while others have been a constant presence and source of guidance for the long haul. I've learned different kinds of things from each one, and there's no doubt in my mind that I wouldn't be where I'm at today without their wisdom.

To explain, I'd like to take each one of these men and explain what I've gotten from letting them teach me for a while.

William Frank Hullander is what it says on my dad's birth certificate. My father, all my grandfathers, and I all have the first name William. Dad goes by Bill, but when he was younger, people called him Billy. In 1964, he was voted king of his high school graduating class, and won "best-looking."

He was a champion water skier, worked third shift at Dupont, started his own carpet company without worrying about a college education, drove a school bus for a decade, and started our family business in 1976. We sold wood burning stoves, hot tubs, hardware, solar panels, swimming pool supplies – whatever it took to get by. Dad saw the opportunity in everything. He was always thinking of us, making ends meet by any means possible.

He's done it all.

Dad was a family man, first and foremost. If there was a peach pie, he'd give himself the last slice. If somebody had to lose sleep, it'd be him. If someone had to go without, dad would assume the responsibility without making a commotion about it. He was a peacemaker, a go-getter, a believer, and a good friend.

My dad grew up watching most of my uncles and cousins drink a lot, make poor decisions, and then become alcoholics. That, along with his faith, is why dad doesn't drink. (I, on the other hand, am a faithful Christian who reaches others over a cocktail – or so I tell myself.)

I remember the one time I even heard dad consider having a beer, I was a young kid and my mom and dad had a fight. They weren't the kind to yell when we could hear, usually, but whatever the issue was, he was mad – and so was mom. So, in the course of them being frustrated at each other,

I heard him say that he was going to get his keys and drive to the liquor store and buy a twelve pack of Coors.

I'd never seen my dad drink. That scared the crap out of me. I don't know what I thought would happen if dad tasted a beer, but clearly, I had to do something about it. I ran out to the barn, grabbed a box of nails, and dumped them out behind the rear tires of his truck.

Dad came out, still huffing mad, saw the nails and put two and two together. He softened. He shrugged, went back in, and told my mother what I'd done, and they made up.

Dad was good at reconciling, even when the problem didn't concern him. When I was in elementary school and he was driving a school bus, he'd make me get up with him at 6am so we could ride together. We'd pick up the high schoolers first, then the junior high students, and last, the elementary-aged kids. Finally, after 2 and a half hours, I got off at Westview Elementary.

But the upshot of this long commute was that I got to watch him at work.

One day I remember, two high school boys, raging with hormones and no idea what to do with them, began to yell and fight on the bus. My dad slowly, calmly pulled the bus over in the parking lot of the Holly Hills neighborhood swimming pool. He said, "Get off the bus," and they got off the bus.

None of us riding knew what was going to happen, but every window was filled with two or three kids trying to see. Dad told the 2 angry high school students, "Go ahead."

They looked at him, confused. So he elaborated.

"You want everyone to know which one of you is toughest. So go ahead and fight each other and we'll find out. Let's see who's tougher. But you can't fight on my bus."

They, and all of us on the bus, were stunned. Before long, dad had them shaking hands, and the bus ride continued without it coming to blows.

When I was 12 years old, we had a different, though maybe not so different, sort of trouble in our neighborhood. Our 2 neighbors, Jeff and Danny, were at each other's throats all the time. Let's just say that one of them was fond of the other man's wife. Their rivalry made all hell break loose on London Lane, where we lived. They would literally shoot at each other from their truck windows as they drove.

With actual guns. Live ammunition. You can see how this would be a problem in a neighborhood full of kids.

We lived in a brick rancher house, and our garage was behind the house, so the driveway went down the side and then hung a left. The reason I'm telling you this is because if you were in the back of the house, you wouldn't know who else was back there until you'd already parked and walked over.

So, one day dad picked up the phone and called Danny.

"Come by the house. I need to talk to you. I'll be out back at the picnic table."

He hung up, then dialed Jeff and said the same thing.

He had one more message then, to my sister and me.

"Go into the house and don't come out."

My sister and I obeyed, which was smart, but we watched events unfold from the back window. Danny arrived first. A couple of minutes later, Jeff showed up. We were wondering what the heck our dad was doing, but he managed to get them both sat down and he started talking. To this day, I don't know what he said to those men, but being my dad, he found a way to broker peace. Danny and Jeff actually shook hands, and there was no more shooting after that. The kids could ride their bikes in the neighborhood once more without fearing for their lives.

Dad is the greatest public servant I've ever known, both in an unofficial capacity and also as an actual representative in local government. He served as county commissioner for 4 terms, and today, he's in his 4th term as county trustee.

When on the county commission, he'd often have to vote several times per meeting. Whenever you had an issue, whether it was on school issues or tax matters, there would usually be two groups in opposition to one another, and your vote was necessarily going to tick off one group or the other. Most commissioners just accepted that fact and expected to leave half of their constituents angry.

Dad didn't see it that way. He'd always try to find a middle ground, or find a way to give each group a little of what they were asking for. It didn't always work out, but they would leave less upset, knowing that their representative was working hard to care for their interests, no matter who they were.

In business, Dad's work set the stage for a family legacy. After the early years of selling anything and everything to anyone with the means and desire to buy it, dad's entrepreneurial spirit kicked into high gear, and he began manufacturing storm windows, then replacement windows, and eventually all kinds of exterior home products. I worked with him from 1991 until 2007 when I bought the company from him. Ultimately, we grew to become one of the largest home improvement companies in the country.

Dad taught me more by his actions than by his words, but what I saw in him has served me well in about everything I've ever attempted.

He taught me a lot about business. He was always beating the drum of working hard and doing what's right. It doesn't matter about profit, convenience, or anything else. You just do what's right, and that's that. His integrity has been my guiding star for many years.

In his footsteps, I also played a role in local politics. I served as chairman of our zoning board for over a decade, and I never forget the way that dad served, trying to find solutions that worked for everybody. I tried to do what he did, and I know that several neighbors who came to our meetings had come ready to fight but left as friends.

Dad helps people constantly. I have countless stories of him being a good Samaritan, and this has made an impression on me to try and do the same.

But of all his guidance, life lessons, and experiences, what he's most proud of is the number of people he's introduced Jesus Christ to. His faith isn't an empty gesture; it's real, and there's going to be a larger crowd in heaven because of Billy Hullander.

I hope to do life half as well as he's done it, and I'm grateful that he provided himself as a role model.

———

Dr. Dave is a man I've described as my second dad, and that's the honest truth. He's a paradoxical mix of humility and brazen confidence. He's serious as a heart attack and yet laughs easily and can take himself lightly, when the time's right.

If I tried to list here all of the things Dave has taught me over the years, it would take a chapter all of its own, and maybe a whole book, so I'll restrict myself to a keen piece of wisdom I learned from him recently.

Dr. Dave's field of expertise is motorcycles, and he's been guiding an annual 4,000-mile motorcycle ride for the last 51 years. Oh, and on this ride, they never touch a freeway or interstate. Over the past few decades, some guys have left, aged out or dropped out, but there are still 8 of them that make the trek, and it's nothing to shake a stick at.

But for how long and difficult the road is, Dr. Dave and his team do it with grins from ear to ear.

I've spent a lot of time at Dr. Dave's, and I mean a lot. I talk with him while he works on bikes, and recently, I was doing just that. His garage was jammed full of motorcycles because it was only a few days before Bike Week in Daytona Beach, and everyone wanted their hogs in tip-top shape. He was hard at work, and I was bitching and carrying on about how much I had on my plate.

Now, I know it might seem ironic to see one man working while another man tells him how hard he, himself, is working – but I really was. I'd let my priorities slide out of whack, and I was slammed. I dragged myself to Dr. Dave for some encouragement or advice – I wasn't even sure. I just knew I was overloaded, and Dr. Dave's a good place to go when you need your head put on straight.

Dr. Dave stopped what he was doing, which immediately made me pay attention, because he's a hard worker and usually keeping busy.

"Come over here and let's sit down," he said, beckoning me over to his counter. I picked a spot, eying all of the memorabilia, old pictures of biker buddies, invoices, parts catalogs, pork rinds, a cordless phone, and then, suddenly, 2 beers. "That one's yours," he said, reaching for the other. He took a sip as he sat on a barstool, pondered his choice of words, and then let me have it.

"Let's say you're in a race, Matt. You can turn the engine on full throttle, and you'll be impressive for a while, but you'll burn out. If you pull it back to ¾, you won't be quite as flashy, but you will finish the race."

I made him repeat it so that I could record it on my phone. Sometimes you hear things like that, things you just can't afford to forget. I wish I'd heard it in 2003 instead of 2023, but you live and you learn.

He was talking about margin. Rest. Two things that don't come naturally to a guy like me. But when I see a great man like Dr. Dave, legendary in his field, still active, productive, and impressive at an advanced age, I think that he's somebody I'd like to emulate.

Dave may be one of the best motorcycle mechanics in the world, but he still takes time to have a beer with friends. He's driven, but he has time for other people's needs too.

He's balanced. Maybe he learned that from riding.

In 2016, I was running hard in business. Hullco was growing at a rapid pace, I had my real estate side hustle going full tilt, I was building a tall commercial building downtown, my 11-year-old daughter was starting junior high and getting dangerously close to her teenage years, and I thought I had to pull it all off while keeping everyone perfectly happy all of the time.

Do you see a breakdown coming? I should have.

One day as I got off of Interstate 24 on the MLK exit ramp, all of the stress and exhaustion I'd kept bottling up came roaring out all at once, and I couldn't fight it any longer. I had to pull over in the City Café parking lot and figure out what on earth had just hit me, and why I suddenly felt like a lunatic.

Was this a panic attack? A nervous breakdown?

Mentally, I was a wreck. I clearly needed some help. I thankfully had enough clarity to google the words "life coach" on my phone. That led me to Jonathan Dunn. He was based out of Florida, and he seemed more than qualified. I saw that he worked with Chik-fil-a locations around the country by supporting and teaching the employees. He'd also worked with the Pentagon, and he even helped stressed-out businessmen like me. I scheduled a call.

I explained my hectic life to JD and the unsustainable pace. I had so many concerns, and it was getting to be too much for me. I wasn't putting my family first, I felt physical pressure on my chest all the time, and obviously I had too much on my plate. I was 43 years old, and I'd always been able to just tough it out before, but this was different. I was in over my head. Something wasn't working, or wouldn't keep working anymore.

JD listened calmly. He was soft-spoken and compassionate as he gave me an analogy many of you will have heard before.

"Matt, you obviously fly on a lot of airplanes. You know when the flight attendant goes through the cabin explaining the safety procedures and demonstrates how to put on your seatbelt?"

"Sure," I said. "I always think it's a stupid waste of time. If you can't buckle a damn seatbelt, how were you smart enough to buy the ticket in the first place, or find your seat?"

"Correct!" he said. "People getting on the plane should already know about the safety features, yet we forget things we should know sometimes. But the seatbelt thing really is obvious; it's what she says after that's so important."

I'll never forget what he told me next.

"She holds up an oxygen mask, Matt, and she explains that if the cabin loses pressure, these will fall from the ceiling so everyone can breathe. But what does she always say about helping other people with their masks?"

"Put your own mask on and ensure air is flowing properly before turning to help others."

"Right again," he said. "Now why do you suppose that is?"

I got chills. I started to see where he was going with this.

"Because you can't help anybody if you're dead."

He was quiet, patiently letting the realization wash over me, which it certainly did.

"I need to take care of myself," I said. "I'm no good to my family if I'm a nervous wreck, no matter how much money I bring in or how large my company gets."

"That's right," he said. "It sounds like you have all sorts of opinions about what other people ought to be doing, and you're doing a lot of good, but you're overloaded and neglecting yourself. It isn't selfishness to keep yourself in good working order, brother. It's necessary if you want to do good things in this world at all."

I felt some conflicting emotions then. I felt a little silly, like this should have been obvious to me. But mostly I felt relief. Because, at bottom, I did know that I needed to take care of myself – but I hadn't thought about it in terms of the oxygen mask analogy. At some point, Matt needed to take care of Matt or there wouldn't be any Matt to take care of anyone else.

Later on, he had me write down the 6 most important things to me in the whole world, and then I had to rank them. Afterwards, feeling good about my list, Jonathan reviewed it and said, "Is this really how you spend your time and money? Does number 1 get the most?"

He wasn't done.

"Do your priorities feel like they are your priorities? Do they know it from your daily actions?"

Finally, he asked me if I wanted more time to spend on my priorities. I said yes. So he challenged me.

"Then logically, you're going to have to start saying no to all the things that didn't make the list."

Harsh for a soft-spoken, kind life coach, I thought. Of course, he was exactly right. Starting the process of reorienting my life saved me a lot of trouble. I'm still working on it today, but I now have the tools and I'm quite a bit better about these things than I ever have been before.

I owe part of this book to JD, honestly. I don't know if I'd be listening to all these podcasts and books, exercising, and taking time to rest if it wasn't for my phone calls with JD.

He's a guide who's helped me navigate some of the tricky waters of my personal life, and I continue to learn from him today.

I've told you already about Clay Mathile and Iams Pet Food. He taught me about vision, and it's because of him that the Aileron Course for Presidents exists. What I haven't told you is that my instructor during my time at Aileron was a great guy named Ed Eppley.

Ed is a fixer, in the best sense of the term. I don't mean that he's one of those shady guys in D.C. who cover up politicians' crimes and indiscretions – he's the type of person who looks at a situation, mulls it over for a moment, and then tells you exactly what the root of the problem is. It's uncanny. He has a rare ability to see through the fog, set aside what's not important, and get to the heart of the matter.

Ed is an author, a podcaster, and a global expert in professional management, sales strategy, and performance management. He's a world-class consultant, and believe me when I tell you that Ed's worked for everybody.

I'm lucky enough to count him as a friend, and he's someone who is a member of my personal tribe, so we keep in touch a good bit and play a lot of golf.

But Ed is one of those rare friends who is also a guide, and I wouldn't be where I am in business if not for his steady approach to management.

On the second day of my time at Aileron, I was wearing an Honor's Course golf shirt, and Ed approached me. I didn't know him personally at the time. We got talking about the game, and I invited him to play the Honor's Course with me. Later, I hired him to consult for my company. Ed helped to teach me the real meaning of vision, mission, values, and a whole lot more. He was eventually on the board of directors at my company, and at the end he helped me sell it. Just today I talked to Ed about my e-commerce venture, and he set up a call with one of his clients on the West Coast. He's been a friend, a mentor, and a big help in my work.

Ed has taught me a lot of things, but underneath every lesson is this:

Keep the main thing, the main thing.

What does that look like? Lose what isn't necessary. Be an essentialist. Don't get distracted. Figure out your primary strength and juice it up to full power. Stay in your lane.

I can't tell you how many guys I've seen over the years who just get distracted. "Shiny object syndrome," they call it. They're like a dog off chasing squirrels. They never seem to catch one, though.

I have a friend who's an engineer, and despite being one of the smartest people I know, he'll never accomplish even 20% of what he's capable of, because he always has to do every part of things himself. He gets delayed and distracted by having to master a new task every step of the way instead of just focusing on what he's best at.

I'd be prone to the same weakness, I think, if it wasn't for people like Ed.

Ed helps me remember not to have too many irons in the fire at once, to put my effort where it will be most effective, and to really vet an opportunity before I dive in.

Every go-getter, self-starter, and excitable entrepreneur, like myself, needs an Ed Eppley.

I've had other guides throughout my life, but these four have probably played the biggest role that way. My dad taught me integrity, compassion, and work ethic. Dr. Dave taught me about friendship, the need for a tribe, and to love what you do. JD grounded me when I needed it, and got me back on track during a difficult time. Ed taught me how to be a better leader, provider, and businessman.

So what kind of a guide do you need? It's different for every person. When I went fishing last, I made sure to hire a guide. Maybe you need to hire a life coach, like JD. Or perhaps you need a business consultant or a personal trainer.

One thing I've learned, competitive as I am, is that you can't do it all yourself. You can't be a professional at everything. So find a professional and let him point you in the right direction.

I'll leave you with one final thought, and forgive me if it's a hair bit morbid. In Nepal they have two terms for people who attempt Mt. Everest without a guide:

Missing or dead.

That's the bad news. The good news is, no matter what mountain is standing in front of you, somebody out there has climbed it before. Now why would you not take a minute to find them and get some insight?

Sometimes we know what we ought to do but we just need reminding, so here's your reminder:

Find a guide.

PRINCIPLE
6

FIND YOUR TRIBE

OR

*Team Up; Birds of a Feather; De-Isolate;
Shoulder to Shoulder; Fill In Your Gaps;
Hunt in a Pack*

I'm feeling straight-forward today, so I won't dress up
the metaphor:

Wolves live longer, hunt better, and recover from sickness
better when they work as a pack.

We love the idea of a lone wolf. Heck, I know a few of
them, and they're good people. So I in no way mean this to
disparage those of my friends who, for one reason or another,
tend to operate alone.

But the verifiable, scientific truth, is that wolves live longer and do better when they're working together.

I don't think people are all that different.

We like to think that we can do it all solo. And hey, maybe for a little while we can. But it's no way to live. In the long term, it's a recipe for stagnation, misery, and frustration.

You need people.

But we're in a weird spot today. We're more connected than ever, but the most isolated we've ever been. Yes, it's a cliché, but it's true. Everybody's got likes on Facebook and followers on TikTok, but few, if any, actual friends.

We're so addicted to our phones that we even prefer them over real people when they're standing right in front of us. We care more about the wifi connection than the human connection.

And we talk about the skyrocketing depression in this country like it's some great mystery. Sure, there's more than one reason for depression, but isolation is the elephant in the room.

But there's a problem, right? This isn't the 1950's. There's no men's club down the street. Entertainment, communication, and door dash are all readily accessible from your couch. Does anybody even go out anymore?

It's a weird world we're living in these days.

You can find a good community at a church, but maybe you aren't religious. Extended family can be helpful, but maybe they live far away, or you don't have any siblings or cousins. So what's the solution? How do we de-isolate?

Join a tribe.

No, this isn't a Mad Max kind of thing where you join a gang, wear trash can lids for clothing, and run wild. This isn't Chicago. (For my Chicago readers, apologies). It's an intentional return to a mode of living that fills some of our deepest needs, and offers us an opportunity to make the world a little better for someone else, while we're at it.

Let me tell you about the first tribe I ever joined.

In 2007, I bought out the family business. Dad had done a great job building something from nothing, and on the solid foundation he laid, I was fixing to put a skyscraper. So I had my nose constantly buried in trade magazines, learned all I could about growth strategies, and I signed up for those industry conferences. You know the ones: big hotel, keynote speaker, and vendors out in the hall trying to sell you stuff. So that's why I found myself at the Hilton in Fort Lauderdale one evening, where I would meet a man who would change my life forever.

The guy who'd invited me to this particular conference had me come out to dinner with his company – they were throwing some shindig for their top dealers – and I sat across from someone they introduced as Steve Taylor. We had a great time that night. We learned about each other's businesses, hobbies, families. It was a great conversation over a shared bottle of wine, half for him and half for me. But since Steve, as it turned out, was a recovered alcoholic, I went ahead and had his half, too.

We hit it off right away.

"Listen, Matt," he said as we finished dessert. "I'm in a peer group. And I'd like to propose you for membership."

"I'm always interested in things that might help me grow my business," I said. "Tell me more."

"Well," he explained, "the way it would work is you'd come to our next meeting, we'll see if we like you; you'll see if you like us. Then you go home and we take a vote and let you know if you're in."

"So it's like a support group for business? Or like a mastermind group?"

He had a twinkle in his eye.

"Yes. We call it 'The Big Dogs.'"

I was hesitant about it at first. Their next meeting was only two weeks away, would require me to travel, and I was up to my neck in work. But, I went home and talked it over with my wife, and I decided to check it out.

Which was good, because I got a phone call the next day from someone who said his name was Scott McClurg.

He explained that he was the president of the peer group that year, and that he understood I'd met someone from the club who proposed me for membership. So we talked some details, and then he said this:

"Say, Matt, my wife comes to these things when she can, but she's a schoolteacher and has to teach, so I'll be flying in alone. Why don't you schedule your flight to come in the same time as me, and I'll pick you up in a rental car, and we can get to know each other a little bit before we get to the meeting."

I thought that sounded alright, so I said yes, and two weeks later, I walked off of the tarmac at the airport, looking around for a person I'd never met before. The only thing I knew was that he was going to have a convertible mustang.

I looked left, looked right, and sure enough, the only convertible mustang was straight ahead, driven by a curly-haired, deep-voiced man arguing with a police officer who wanted him to move his car.

Scott apparently was a retired firefighter, and he was trying to show the cop his badge, and the cop was telling him that he didn't give a damn if he was a firefighter or Harriet Tubman, he had to move.

So I walked up to the car, where this guy that I'm hoping is the person who's supposed to be picking me up, is now actually shouting back and forth with this police officer. I put my suitcase in the backseat; didn't say a word. I opened the door; nobody's so much as glanced at me. I got in and put my seatbelt on, and then the driver tells that police officer two words before peeling out of there. As we drove off, he stuck his hand out and said, "Hey, I'm Scott."

And the two words he said to the police officer, by the way, were not "Happy Birthday," if you get my drift.

So that's how I met Scott, with whom I drove for the next two hours across a place actually called "Alligator Alley." We had some laughs, got to know each other a bit, and by the time we got to the hotel – a pricey one – we decided to share a room and save a couple grand each. We hit up the gym before the meeting, and I was struck by how easy it was to get along with this guy and the guy who nominated me for membership in the first place.

At the actual meeting, my first time seeing "The Big Dogs" all together, things started to make sense. These guys were slapping backs, catching up, laughing. They'd all become good friends through this business group.

But it wasn't all fun and games. During the meeting, they were grilling each other on their financials, grilling each other on strategy, checking up on each other's progress from the last time they'd gotten together, and providing advice and actual help.

They were functioning like a body, a network that made every part better. I'd never seen anything quite like it in action before.

I'll save you the suspense. I got voted in before the meeting was over, while I'd gone to the restroom. Over the next several years, I'd go to Scott if I was having a production problem in my business, because he was great at production. But if Alan was having trouble with his marketing, he'd come to me, because that's where I excel. We knew each other's enterprises so well, that when one of our members got cancer in 2015, we all took turns flying out to his home and running his business for him, about a month at a time each. When he finally got through the treatments and was ready to get back to life, his work was still there for him.

When I joined the group, my remodeling company was doing $4.5 million in sales. After a few years being pushed, prodded, and helped by The Big Dogs, I was doing $20 million.

There's an old expression that says, "A rising tide lifts all ships." Boy, is that true.

But this isn't a business book, and a tribe doesn't have to be all about business. So to that end, I want to tell you about another tribe – an unofficial one, as it turns out. And it's led by a world-renowned tradesman known as Dr. Dave, who I mentioned briefly in the last chapter.

David Clemmons works exclusively on Harley-Davidson motorcycles, and his place, Dr. Dave's Repair Shop, is one of the best there is. He himself is considered one of the best mechanics in the country. At his shop, he works on bikes for policemen, Hell's Angels, businessmen, and whoever else rolls in. But every Wednesday at 5 o'clock, Dave stops working and opens up the doors to a converted chicken house, complete with classic motorcycles, a bar, and memorabilia hanging on the walls.

It's a killer man cave.

Dr. Dave's tribe is an informal one. Not too many rules or a club charter or anything like that. If you know Dave, or if one of his friends invites you, you can come and hang out on a Wednesday, provided that you bring domestic lite beer. They won't let you in without it. And none of that "froo-froo stuff," as Dave says. I'd personally rather sip on a hazy IPA, but when I go see Dave, I bring Miller Lite. He's old school, and it's his tribe after all.

Dave's crowd is an eclectic bunch. There are ex-cons and cops, tattoos, pony tails, three-piece suits, ripped jeans, beards, and clean-shaven faces. There are two guys named Ray (Old Ray and Ray-Ray), and in decades, I have never once seen Old Ray wearing anything besides overalls. Some other members are called Buggs, Hog Dawg, Chief, and Conehead. And me, everyone just calls me "Hey, Buddy."

With all of the peculiarities I've mentioned, you might be tempted to write this group of guys off as a bunch of good ol' boys chewing the fat and wasting time. But you'd be wrong. Because, aside from the rich relationships that have formed over the years, these men help each other. We all help each other.

When Old Ray goes out of town, Dave pays his bills, collects rent from his tenants, and checks on his house. When a storm took down trees at Dr Dave's, we all showed up with chainsaws. When Conehead passed away, the group was there for his widow. When the Sheriff's department does Toy's for Tots at Christmas, we all show up.

Not bad for a group for which the membership requirements are "know somebody" and "bring lite beer." But there are unwritten rules in life as well as the written kind, and we don't need an NDA to keep each other's secrets. These men live shoulder to shoulder, and it's a great deal easier to succeed in all walks of life when you know you have some brothers or sisters watching your back.

Not to put too fine a point on it, but I'd like this for you. For whatever my opinion counts, I'm going to come out and say it directly: you need a tribe.

I'm more the storytelling type than the "sit down and listen to the rules" type, but in this case, it's helpful to understand some of the particulars for how you can set up a tribe of your own. You don't have to do things my way, and there may be a tribe in your community that already exists, and you can jump on in with them. But if you don't have something like that, listen to how I put this principle into practice.

I'm still in the Big Dogs group, even though I sold my business. And I still go and hang out with Dr. Dave and Hog Dog from time to time. But in recent years, I've set up a formalized tribe that relates to all aspects of life. We sign NDAs, so that people feel more comfortable opening up about sensitive issues. We have rules for membership and for losing membership. We all get together at particular times, but we are in contact throughout the year. And the purpose of the whole thing is to have a group that goes through life together, as brothers-in-arms, help when you need it, and accountability.

If that word, accountability, is a trigger for you, more on that later. But first, take a look at this one-sheeter that I've developed, which we fill out before each time we get together.

The hope is that each one of us could show up with this sheet all filled in with 10's, saying that everything is perfect and we're living up to our full potential. But, as that just plain isn't going to happen, we talk through our successes and failures, list our problems, ask for advice, share our aspirations, and report on progress. Take a look at the sheet:

Spring Meeting   T.O.M.

Name :
Age ;

MONEY SECTION
Total Assets : $
Total Liabilities : $ 5 Years from now New Worth Goal : $
Net Balance (Net Worth) : $ Yearly Income Goal: $
How is your net worth diversified (roughly, what buckets are you invested in ?) :

_____

Areas of concern about money:

_____

HEALTH SECTION
Weight :   5 Year Goal :
Body Fat % :   5 Year Goal :
Life Expectancy :
Area of concern about health :

_____

LIFE HAPPINESS SECTION
Rate the following from 1 to 10 (1 sucks and 10 is great)
Love for work _____   Romance _____   Friends _____   Hobbies _____
Parents _____   Siblings _____   Children _____   Travel _____
Chill Time _____   Risk / Excitement _____ Giving Back _____
Personal Growth _____ Future Planning _____   Relationship with God _____
How can you be a better Christian ?

_____

FUTURE AND WINS
What are your top 3 wins YTD ?   What Are Your Top 3 Goals ?
1.   1.
2.   2.
3.   3.

What are your future / longterm goals ?
1.
2.
3.

What can the tribe help you with ?

Here's the format we've developed:

- Membership is currently at 7, and we've capped it at a maximum of 8.
- Any member can propose a new member, but for that person to get voted it, the group has to agree unanimously.
- You can be asked to leave the group for breaking trust, sharing private information with others outside the tribe, consistently being a jerk, missing two meetings in a row, or never making progress on the issues you bring to the table.
- Twice a year (midwinter and midsummer), we fly to a member's home city, and he hosts (we rotate this responsibility). We spend two to three days together in fellowship, intensive community, and have a little bit of fun.
- The first meeting is members only, where we report on our one-sheet and how we're doing, what we're struggling with, and where we need help.
- The second meeting is with our spouses
- The host member sets up meals and activities for us to do together afterwards.
- We keep off of our phones and focus on being in the moment together.

I hosted our last get-together here in Tennessee. We met in my basement for our meetings, had some great dinners together, and I set up a full-body scan where we would each get a complete work-up of our health from a doctor buddy of mine.

One of the guys in my tribe was told by the doctor that if he didn't get his body fat percentage down and lose some serious weight, it was only a matter of time before the heart attack showed up. It was the wake-up call he'd been needing, and it lit a fire under him. Another guy in the group was diagnosed with ADD – which I didn't think was a real thing until I was diagnosed with it a couple of years ago. I was able to share a specialist's information with the guy in my tribe, as well as some techniques and practices that have helped me.

This time around, we had a little bit of a focus on health because of the activities I scheduled. After all, if you have the perfect marriage, great kids, an incredible business or job, and a meaningful place in the community, but you die because you've neglected your body, that sort of robs you of the other stuff, doesn't it?

But this is the beauty of our group. When we sat down for that first meeting, each guy had an hour to talk through their sheet. Advice and help came informally throughout the rest of the trip, but for that hour, each of us had a chance to really open up and do an audit on our lives. When you took a glance at the one-sheeter I pasted in here, you might have thought it silly to reduce something like "Planning for the Future" to a single number you're ranking yourself with. But in doing so, it turns into talking about estate planning, spirituality, vision, and the like. None of these discussions would have happened if we didn't write a number on the line.

Some guys needed help with their marriage, but their physical health and finances were doing well. Some guys had a wonderful marriage, and they were pretty healthy, but their finances needed attention. It's different for everyone, but on the balance, as a tribe, we are all stronger because of each other's strengths, and because of the (here's that word again) accountability.

Now, some people don't like this word. It feels like a disappointed teacher is breathing down your neck, maybe. But having accountability hacks a flaw in us. To explain this, I have to once again take a swipe at the "goal setting" mindset.

Your brain runs on a number of neurochemicals that make you feel happy, sad, close to a loved one, etc. This isn't a neuroscience book, and I can barely pronounce "serotonin," so we won't get hung up on the details. But what's important to know is that a whole part of your brain is what they call the "reward center" which basically makes you feel like you're successful and doing a good job. That reward center runs on a neurochemical called "dopamine." And your body releases dopamine when you achieve something good and get recognition for it. That way, your brain says "Hey, this was a good thing. We should do it more often."

The problem is, accomplishment is not the only thing that releases dopamine. You actually get the same hit of that stuff when you share your goals. Not only when you actually achieve them, but just by speaking them aloud, you get that sense of reward.

Why is that a problem? Because research shows that this tends to make people less effective at finishing what they set out to do, since their brains have already gotten the reward.

I've said it before, and I'll say it a couple more times before we're done: We need accountability.

If we were honest with ourselves and someone asked how we were doing, the "goals" version of us would respond with, "Great! I thought about going for a run this morning. I imagined what it would be like if I skipped my coffee habit (I didn't), and I alllllllmost prayed."

Pathetic, right? We need accountability.

So, in our group, what we're aiming at naturally comes up. But we don't slap each other on the back for goals, the way you do in polite conversation. Nobody says, "Oh, you'd like to run a marathon? That's amazing. Good for you. I could never do that." We discuss if it's a good and helpful thing to be putting energy towards, and then we ask for their plan of action. At the next meeting, we say "Did you run that marathon? Has your training improved? What are your numbers?"

We don't celebrate goals in our tribe, we celebrate progress. It's a shift in thinking, but it is a profound help to us in all areas of life.

Maybe this type of intensive self-improvement group is for you. Or you might prefer a couples group that focuses more on relationships, or a Bible-study life group that puts the center on spiritual growth, or perhaps you'd like to be in a business peer group like The Big Dogs. At the end of the day, no matter what type of tribe you have, the friendships that form are the real reason to do it.

We've debased the word "friend" in the modern era. You meet someone at an office party and laugh at a few of her jokes, and all the sudden we say she's a "friend." But a friend is something deeper. Friends help each other. And if you can find a few good friends, real friends, then life just goes to another level. We're starved for it, I think.

A tribe is helpful, of course, and it really can make you a better person. But a word of caution about all of this.

You are the sum of the five closest people around you, as Jim Rohn said, and sometimes you need to fire somebody from your group. Don't do this willy-nilly, and it doesn't have to always be a big dramatic rejection. But focus on who you can help and be helped by. Not everyone wants to get better. Some people are content to drag others down, so there are a few more swine down in the mud for company. Harsh words, but true.

And finding the right tribe can often be an exercise in trial and error. Don't be surprised if it doesn't work out the first couple of times you give it a shot. Keep at it. Landing in a real, effective tribe is worth all the headache of getting there.

See, the secret to this life is that people are the real treasure.

PRINCIPLE
7

GET FIT, STAY FIT

OR

You Can't Accomplish Your Vision if You're Dead; Feel Better to Do Better; The Shortest Chapter in this Book

Let's make this one short and sweet.

I'm not a doctor, a nutritionist, or a personal trainer. But I've got some common sense, and here's something I've learned:

You can have all of your priorities straight.

You can have a clear vision.

You can have a mindset for success.

You can have a tribe and a guide to help you.

You can have all of the talent and drive in the world.

But if you have a heart attack at 40, and they bury you 6 feet under, none of the rest of that stuff is going to help you.

Going to the gym is not the most important thing in the world, but your physical health is what allows you to be effective in the world. It's important. When I work out in the morning, I feel better all day. When I move, my arthritis hurts less and I have more energy.

Self-discipline, especially in this area, expands our capacity. We all struggle with things that go against growing in self-discipline, but we can overcome them. What are the things that rob you of your self-discipline? Is it Instagram, Netflix, too much screen time, that bag of chips, hitting the snooze alarm, or that third bourbon?

The most successful people do the highest impact things possible at any given moment or any given day. For me, I have to schedule it. I put the most important things on my calendar. I know when I'm going to work out, so I lay my clothes out the night before. Even these small actions towards keeping our priorities creates momentum.

People worry about motivation with a fitness plan. The key is stick to it, and keep your momentum.

This is the shortest chapter, but certainly not the least important. So here is my message: spend some time figuring out how to be fit.

We have a great advantage over our parents' generation in that we've got some amazing technological advancements in medicine and health. There's cryotherapy, infrared saunas, red light therapy, full body scans, hormone replacement therapy, biohacking, and all sorts of other helpful tools for telling us what to look out for, and how to get better. My wife and I do them all.

Don't neglect your health. It will catch up to you. We're all getting older, and your body will thank you for that daily walk, watching what you eat, or taking the medication you need.

You started aging the day you were born, so don't let yourself get taken out of the race early. Even if this isn't your area of comfort, and even if it's going to be hard.

Get fit and stay fit.

PRINCIPLE
8

PLAN TO FAIL

OR

*Fall Forward; Don't Panic; Tesla Lost, Too;
Don't Get Bitter, Get Better; The Upside;
God's Plan Ain't Your Plan*

This is my humble story of how I ran for mayor of Hamilton County, Tennessee.

Spoiler alert, I didn't win. Losing was not in my plan. But as I look at my life since then, I think it was in God's plan. In fact, I know it was, and the principle here is that we can't avoid failure completely. So we might as well embrace that failures can sometimes happen on purpose, or at least they happen for a reason. Fortunately, failures can lead to success. And if we learn from the experience, failure can be more valuable than an instance of success in the long run.

I decided to run for mayor in 2021 with good intentions and maybe not as much reflection as I ought to have given it. I had just sold my business, which had taken up most of my time for most of my life, and I was looking for something to do. My dad was an elected official, and the mayor's office was right across the hall from his office, and I thought it'd be nice to spend more time with him. But if I'm being honest, I felt led to do the mayor's race so I could give back and make Hamilton County better.

I'd had success. My dad was a public servant, and I thought if I'm half as good as him, I'll do a great job as mayor. It didn't hurt that I'd had private meetings with the then current mayor, and he was behind me. Nearly every county commissioner was behind me. Actually, nearly every elected official was behind me.

I had endorsements from our congressman, our sheriff, and a bunch of other important guys in Hamilton County.

I paid for surveys to be done, and between the ones I set up and the local news' polls, I was way up going in. I was at something like 70% and the clear favorite early on. I had good name recognition, and, as I had been in a series of TV ads for quite a few years, my face was even familiar a good chunk of the town. A lot of people knew me personally, also.

Honestly, it seemed like the race wasn't going to be that hard.

I want to be careful here, because I don't want to get anybody fired up or cause any grumblings around town. But the race got dirty, and I didn't like that.

My opponents released mass-mailing attack ads against me that painted me like I was an evil villain who exploited the people who'd worked for me. They blacked out my eyes. They found the one and only time I'd had a wage and labor audit in 40 plus years of business and made it sound like I was using and abusing this employee of mine. All that happened was I was being nice and letting him work some overtime that he asked for, and I let him drive a company vehicle home, so technically that made him still on the clock for his commute. I ended up writing him a check for a few thousand dollars, and that was it.

But they dredged that up and misinterpreted everything.

"Matt Hullander is a horrible boss – what will he be like as our mayor?"

"Matt Hullander uses people. Would you want to work for him? So why would you vote for him?"

That kind of thing.

Not much gets under your skin more than being told you're doing something wrong when you've tried so hard to do it right. I've paid for employees' personal expenses – funerals, vehicles, birthdays, graduation gifts. I've lost sleep trying to figure out how to keep tough situations in business from affecting my employees. I've written cards and letters, made myself available, and prayed for the people I've hired over the years.

I didn't appreciate the lies being told about me. But they were working. Public opinion started to turn, late in the race.

I had a political consultant from Nashville, and he came to me with two commercials already produced about my main opponents, and they were pretty bad.

"(Name censored) has family ties to George Soros."

"...has never had a job."

"...is not a real member of the party."

"...has very shady income sources."

"...has had four different spouses."

"...has piles of unpaid bills."

"...was evicted for non-payment."

You get the idea. They were damning ads, and they made a point as to the fitness of my opponents for office.

My consultant said, "Run these two commercials, and you're a shoo-in." I believe he was right.

But I kept looking at my daughter, Reese and thinking, "I don't want her to see me slinging mud at people. One of these people lived down the street from my parents. The other I see around town all the time."

I couldn't bring myself to do it. I didn't want to play that way.

My consultant got mad. He didn't like me turning down good material to damage my opponents' campaigns, but it was my call.

Their mud-slinging was working, and I went out and tried to have a positive campaign that focused on what I wanted to do, instead of insulting the others in the race.

A couple of months before election day, I sat down with Charlie Kirk, who my pastor had gotten to come and visit our church, to ask his advice on the situation about the attack ads.

He said, "You have to be in the arena to make change, and that means you have to win."

I said, "But isn't smearing the others dirty politics?"

"Are the accusations in the ads your consultant gave you true?"

I nodded.

"Then there's your answer," he said.

Maybe I should have listened to him, but I had a picture of the sort of guy I wanted to be. And that guy wouldn't have run those ads.

The night of the election, I'd booked the Chattanoogan Hotel for my victory party, but the early results didn't look good.

My consultant, who was still mad at me, said, "How many speeches did you write, Matt?"

"Just one," I said.

"You'd best start working on a concession speech, then," he said. "Because tonight isn't going to be your night." He started cussing then, in front of my family, and saying I should have let him run his commercials, but I kicked him out of my room and asked him to leave the hotel. You shouldn't talk that way in front of my wife and daughter. It got me upset.

We sat back down in the awkward silence and waited for the final results.

In the end, it came down to only a few hundred votes. I very likely would have won if I had responded to the attack ads with attack ads of my own. I never went low. I took the high road, and I lost because I did.

That gave the loss another dimension. I felt like it was my fault, but I was conflicted. I was frustrated, too, about what it takes to win just a local race in politics, and how badly we treat each other.

Looking back, I thought maybe I should have just toughened up and given it to them, but I kept my integrity.

You've heard it said, "No wonder good people don't run for public office." I now see why.

I lost my identity, though.

I felt like I was drifting, like I didn't have a purpose. Selling my business was a big win, but it had also been a huge part of my life, and now that was gone. I thought I'd work across the hall from my dad, serving the place I'd grown up in, but I lost. My daughter was growing up and I knew it wouldn't be long until she was graduating high school and leaving the house.

I felt like a failure, and I didn't know what to do.

Thankfully, I didn't give up or drown my sorrows in a bottle. I was real disappointed for a long while, and I did a lot of soul-searching, but as we've discussed earlier in this book, good things came out of it. I was able to redefine my metrics for success in the next stage of my life. I reprioritized the things that matter most to me, like my faith and my family. I started focusing on self-improvement and got healthier in mind and body. I made new connections at a concert in Arizona of all places, and a couple of years later I'm running a nationwide e-commerce company and loving my new life.

Would I be happier if I had won that mayor's race? I can't honestly say. I don't know what could have been, but I do know that God had other plans.

And that's important to remember when something doesn't work out. God had other plans.

I don't know if I'd have gone on this journey of self-discovery and new disciplines without failing at the mayor's race. On the other side, I can see that I've gotten plenty out of losing.

When you think of it, that isn't so bad.

———————————————————

In Greg McKeown's book Essentialism, he says this:

"Admit failure to begin success. I remember a friend who could never stop to ask for directions, because he could never admit he was lost. So we would waste time and energy driving around in circles, getting nowhere... Only when we admit we have made a mistake can we make [it] a part of our past. When we remain in denial, on the other hand, we continue to circle pointlessly. There should be no shame in admitting to a mistake. After all, we are only admitting that we are now wiser than we once were."

Losing the mayor's race isn't the only time I've failed at something important or admit that I'd made a mistake. But once again, when I look in the rearview mirror, the failure paved the way for a much bigger success.

I wouldn't trade it.

At the writing of this book, I have been married to Jenny, the love of my life, for 22 years, but most people don't know that I was previously married. Yes, I've been divorced. The big "D word."

It's water way under the bridge now, and even if it wasn't, I don't think it's right for me to sit here and list the reasons my first marriage didn't work out. But take my word for it that it was broken, and I knew it.

A great friend of my father's and a great friend of mine, Mike Carter, gave his testimony at my church one Sunday while all of this was going on. Mike was an impressive, upstanding guy. He was a state representative for Tennessee, but in his early days, he was a lawyer. He told us that many people used to come to him wanting a divorce. He kept a Bible on the corner of his desk, however, and on those convictions, he saved many of those marriages that were in danger. He told those stories during church, and I felt guilty.

I was really unhappy, and the relationship was not right, but I thought God wanted me to stay married. I thought it would be wrong to get divorced under any circumstances.

Well, one morning Mike called me.

I didn't call him – he called me.

Mike said, "Matt, As soon as I woke up this morning I had you on my mind."

Crazy how the big man works – and I don't mean Mike.

I explained my entire situation to Mike, and, in a sense, I got his permission to take the divorce route. I didn't have much at the time. My ex-wife and I went through mediation, and everything got settled.

I owed her $12,000, her Toyota Camry, and the refrigerator. Just those three things. The problem was that I didn't have the first one.

My best friend Bobby Winnie ran a finance company, so I thought I'd hit him up to see if I could get a $12,000 loan. I met Bobby for the first time while tailgating at a Tennessee football game over a Miller Lite, and we've since tailgated at hundreds of Tennessee events. I thought he was someone who would be understanding and help me out. I went to his office, not quite hat in hand, but still needing a hand.

At Bobby's office, there was a very attractive, then-19-year-old with a nose ring who worked for him. I made sure to meet her that day. 24 years later Jenny still puts up with me, and we're still in love.

Crazy how the big man works.

I've shared two stories so far, and I have a few more. So far there's a theme:

Lose to win.

Lose a good thing, win something greater.

Failures like those can be hard to deal with in the moment, but ultimately, they aren't hard to accept because they panned out.

But not all failure is like that. Sometimes there is no upside, or at least, there is no upside that we can see. Whoever said, "No bad days," might have had a point, but they were also lying.

I've had a few bad days.

Once, when my daughter was 6 and a half years old, Jenny and I took her to a winter clothes store called "Dodge City" because we were going to take a Christmas trip to visit my sister in Wyoming. So we went in to buy ski pants or whatever, and we saw a man with two cocker-spaniels. My daughter loved dogs, and we asked the guy if she could play with them. He said yes.

I thought I was a great dad in that moment, getting her some clothes while she was down on the floor playing with a couple of dogs and their toys. And all of it would have been fine, except at the checkout, the store clerk had forgotten to take one of the security clips off of the pants we bought, and the alarm went off, which spooked one of the dogs.

Reese was down petting it, right close to its face, and it went after her. I saw lots of blood. It was awful. I dropped my bags and kicked the dog as fast as I could, and I picked up my little girl to run her to the car. The dog had chewed her face pretty good, and there was a hole through her cheek the size of a quarter. I couldn't believe this was happening after things were so peaceful a second ago. She howled and cried and we were terrified for her.

She got thirty-some-odd stitches on the outside, and another thirty on the inside. They had to correct where her jaw tore away from the bone. It was horrific.

I don't know what the upside to that was. I don't know if there was one. My 6-year-old got traumatized and seriously injured on a family outing, and I had said she could play with the stupid dogs.

She's beautiful, though, and so in that sense it turned out. Her wounds healed. She stayed away from dogs for a few years. Her mom and I were more careful about animals being around her after that, but time heals all wounds, and now, Reese loves our golden doodle Bindi.

But that was a bad day.

I had another bad day in 2011.

We were glued to the TV set. Earlier in the day, tornados had ripped across the South, leaving a trail of destruction and death in Tuscaloosa, Alabama and all through Georgia. I had just built a new house on our family farm, and we'd only been living there for 3 weeks, but already it looked like our new home might be in danger. Originally, they estimated this big storm would hit southeast of us in Cohutta, Georgia, but they were wrong.

The tornado hit Hullander Farm head-on at 7:58pm. It was an F-5, and the wind speed clocked in at 201mph. I'd gotten Jenny and my daughter Reese in the center of the house in our master closet, but my dumb ass went to look out the window. I couldn't help it.

I saw dozens of huge mature pine trees crash down 50 yards from my house. It was over in only a second. We had survived. Others were not so lucky. It was getting dark, but we had no power and the house was filled with the smell of propane. My parents, who lived next door, ran over to check on us. More storms were approaching, so my family and I, along with some neighbors, got in my parents' basement and didn't come out until around midnight. We turned on some old flashlights to look into the darkness.

We couldn't believe our eyes.

It was chaos. My dad had 3 barns before the tornado. They were gone. Vehicles had been tossed around like Frisbees. Power lines and trees were everywhere. I had left my front door open to let the propane escape, and now that brand-new home was filled with every limb and leaf in the neighborhood. I couldn't see the floor in my house.

The next several weeks did show me the heart of my friends and neighbors, however. The community rallied together, and the outpouring of help was amazing.

But the loss was heavy.

240 people died that day from those tornados. 2 of my cousins, 2 of Jenny's cousins, and 1 employee, Josh Poe.

That was the second worse day of my life.

My sister Mandy got married in 2007 on my birthday, June 9th at Turpin Meadows Ranch in Jackson, Wyoming. That was a good day. My new brother-in-law Chris Horne was a cool dude, and I was glad to have him in the family. He played guitar and treated my sister right. He was a good-looking guy with a natural likability. He and my sister were both school teachers living in Jackson at the time, but they had big plans.

They wanted to start a family, so as to prepare the way for my future nieces and nephews, Chris took a better paying job as a charter school director in Cashiers, North Carolina. I remember helping them move into their new place, their forever home.

It was picture perfect.

Chris and Mandy had Thanksgiving week off that year, so they planned a trip to Baja in Mexico. They wanted to catch up with some of their teacher friends at a surf camp down there and it seemed like a fun little vacation. 4 days in Baja, then drive down to Cabo for 2 more, and fly home.

Back in Chattanooga, I was having a normal Wednesday while they were traveling. It was the day before Thanksgiving, I'd been to lunch, and I was driving back to work when I got a phone call from my mother.

I could hardly understand her. She was sobbing uncontrollably, but I was able to make out two things:

"Mandy and Chris were in a wreck."

And

"Chris has died."

I was able to get more of the story from my dad, and it was ugly.

There were four people in a car that crossed the center line on Federal Highway 1, just 10 miles outside of Cabo, which rammed into my sister's car. 3 People in the car wreck died, but Mandy lived. She was rushed to the nearest hospital.

I ran to my parents' house, trying to process what to do and how to help, all while coping with the loss of my brother-in-law and worried sick for my sister. We didn't know where her friends were, how to contact her or anyone else, or even if she was going to make it.

We didn't know anything.

I was powerless.

In desperation, I logged into my sister's email account and tried everything I could think of for her password.

Her first car was an Accord. That wasn't it. We grew up on London Lane. That wasn't it. Her dog's name was Sedona.

And that was it.

I found her itinerary and the surf camp in Baja. I called and tried to explain who my sister was. The lady on the phone said she knew her, and she told me that her friends were still at the camp. She put me on hold, and then, only a couple of hours after I'd had to tell Chris' dad that his son had died, I had to tell Mandy's best friends the same news, and that Mandy was in trouble.

It was the worst day of my life. It was a bad day. A failure.

And it didn't matter that I hadn't caused it. It still felt like a failure, like something that shouldn't happen. And every minute I didn't have some control over getting my sister to safety felt like a personal failure.

We got hold of the U.S. Embassy, finally, and the guy on the phone wasn't enthusiastic.

"Mr. Hullander," he said, sounding tired, "One American dies down here every day. These yahoos don't know how to drive in this country. And good luck trying to deal with them – the only way you'll get your brother-in-law's body back is if they cremate him."

It was not an encouraging call.

The hospital that had my sister finally contacted us. They said, "She needs to be airlifted to El Paso, but we're not letting her go until you send us $20,000."

Sounds legit, right? But what choice did I have? I sent them my credit card and faxed a signature.

Then the air ambulance people called and said, "We're not bringing her to El Paso until you give us $25,000."

So I had to drive back to my office while on the phone with the manager at my bank, trying to talk him into raising my limit. It was a disaster. How many more people had to be paid large sums of money before my sister was safe?

I helped my parents find a chartered plane, and they got to El Paso before my sister did. They were with her when they rolled her into University Medical Center, covered with injuries both internal and external. She was awake, though, and she asked my mom where Chris was.

What do you say?

When she didn't really answer, Mandy said, "Mom, I know Chris has died, but I need to hear it from someone. Please tell me."

The charter plane pilots were very kind, and they agreed to wait in Texas until Mandy was cleared to travel. They waited 3 days and missed Thanksgiving, but I was grateful, because they brought my family back to Tennessee.

Mandy had 3 broken ribs, a broken pelvis, a fractured foot, stitches in 3 places on her face, and a subdermal hematoma, but she eventually healed is doing well physically today. Chris' father was able to bring his son's ashes home in his lap on a Delta flight the next week.

After that, there was a lot of hurt, and 3 funerals – 1 in Cashiers, North Carolina, 1 in Jackson, Wyoming, and 1 in Alexandria, Virginia, where Chris was from.

So what was the upside in that? What was the "greater win" on the other side of the loss?

I don't know. It doesn't seem like there was one. Sometimes something really is just tragedy all the way around.

———————

Life sucks some days, but the daily climb must continue. Challenges and difficulties are inevitable parts of life, but they can also be for growth and transformation if we stay humble and don't give up. We can't wallow in pity or the pain of the past forever. The sun keeps rising every day, and we must rise with it.

After bad things happen it's hard to not worry. I'm terrible at this, but I continue to remind myself that God's in charge. We must believe in ourselves and our abilities, and never let fear or doubt hold us back.

When you encounter difficulties, instead of giving up, take a deep breath and remind yourself that you have the strength and determination to overcome them and keep pressing forward every day. We can't sit in the basement and hide from the world, no matter how unfair the failure.

If you face your difficulties head-on, stay positive, and never give up, then even the worst that life has to throw at you won't keep you down forever.

And if you can't be kept down, you'll rise.

The tragedies will define your character, and make you more compassionate.

The failures that came from your mistakes will become lessons, and you'll be wiser.

The bad luck that ruins your plans will just be one more step in the journey to a better you.

You can't avoid failure, loss, or pain, but you can take the daily climb, and rise above the clouds again, every day.

PRINCIPLE
9

PURPOSE

OR

The One Thing; Define Yourself;
The Why, Aimless Ain't Painless;
What Are You Here For?

Did you ever see the movie *City Slickers*, with Billy Crystal?

It's about a nearly-middle-aged guy named Mitch, who feels lost. He loves his wife and kids, but he's bored with his work and feeling aimless in life. So, his best friends buy him a vacation in New Mexico where you work on a ranch and then drive real cattle with real cowboys.

At one point, Billy Crystal is riding alone with Curly, the tough old cowboy that has them all amazed. Billy Crystal doesn't understand him, and asks him why he never settled down.

"A cowboy leads a different kind of life... when there were cowboys. We're a dying breed. Still means something to me, though. In a couple of days, we'll move this herd across the river, drive 'em through the valley. There's nothing like bringing in a herd."

Billy Crystal nods along.

"See, now that's great. Your life makes sense to you."

Curly scoffs, then chuckles.

"What's so funny?" Crystal asks.

"You city people worry about a lot of shit."

"Shit?" Crystal replies. "My wife basically told me she doesn't want me around."

"Is she a redhead," Curly asks, raising his eyebrows.

Curly likes redheads.

Crystal frowns.

"I'm just saying..." Curly says, smiling. "How old are you?" the old cowboy asks, after a minute. "38?"

"39."

Curly scoffs again.

"Y'all come up here about the same age. Same problems. Spend about 50 weeks a year getting' knots in your rope. Then you think two weeks here'll untie 'em for you. None of you get it. Do you know what the secret to life is?"

"No. What?"

Curly holds up one finger.

"This."

Crystal's character frowns.

"Your finger?"

"One thing. Just one thing," Curly explains. "You stick to that and everything else don't mean shit."

"That's great," Crystal says. "But what's the one thing?"

"That's what you gotta figure out," Curly replies.

———

What is your one thing?

Remember, "priority" used to only refer to one idea. There weren't "priorities;" you had your priority. It's like that with purpose. What is your one thing?

People get this wrong a lot of ways.

They'll say things like, "My purpose is to lose weight."

Really? That's why God put you on this earth? How much weight you did or did not lose is how you'll be remembered when you're gone? No. Losing weight is your intention. It's a goal, and it's probably even a good goal. But it isn't your purpose.

Your purpose is something that runs through your whole life, and in some way or another, affects everything you do.

My purpose is something I'm still working on defining, exactly, but I've got it narrowed down. Articulating your purpose is something that can take a while, but it's worth doing.

For me, I am a connector. I get people into a better spot to accomplish their endeavors, and, without being boastful, connecting people is what I do multiple times a day. People know to come to me when they need the right business partner, marketing guy, advice about fundraising, whatever. I know a lot of folks, and I help them find where they're needed.

But even this isn't my purpose.

As I go deeper, I think what underlines it all is that I just like improvement. I like to get stuff done better and quicker. I don't like to waste time.

That's why I connect people, in fact. When someone comes to me with an issue, I don't have to sit there and solve it for them, go back and research, and bang my head against a wall. I just pick up my phone and call the person who's best suited to help.

And it's true, some people are influencers, and some really aren't, aside from a small circle, maybe. God has chosen to bless me with a lot of friends, and so linking people up is just part of the way I go about making things better and quicker.

This was even our slogan at my company for a while: #MakeItBetter.

I'm still working on it, and if you asked me what my purpose is five years from now, maybe I'd give you a different answer. After I lost the mayor's race and sold my business, I felt a little bit like Billy Crystal did in City Slickers, but I leaned into the process, and I'm figuring it out.

Purpose isn't something that falls right into your lap. Sometimes, maybe it does, but most of the time I think you have to go looking for it.

Purpose is what'll keep you going on hard days, when it seems like you're stuck in the mud and spinning your wheels. It's your "why." And we all need a why.

So I'll ask you again: What is the one thing in your life that you could give everything else up for? What matters more than anything else?

What is your one thing?

Now, here's the other half of the idea that balances it all out:

Can we ever really zero in on our purpose all of the way? Is "purpose" a real thing that's running around out there somewhere, waiting to be found? There are some helpful questions we can ask ourselves to get close, but it's worth wondering whether this is a journey or a destination.

In the self-help world, everyone asks, "What is my life's purpose?" and "How do I find my purpose?" They ask like it's sitting out there under a rock or something.

"Here, Purpose, Purpose..."

If you want to know life's purpose, try to answer this question:

"How can I use my time in a way that feels important to me?"

Young adults may ask "What should I do with my life?" and middle-aged people say, "I haven't found my purpose yet." Really what they want to know is how to use their time well.

How to spend your time is a very important question, and it's not always easy to answer. It was easy from my friend Tim to answer. His purpose is to share Jesus with others. And boy, does he do it.

What about you? As you stand in front of the mirror every day, ask yourself, "If this was my last day on earth, would I feel good about what I'm doing today?" What would you answer?

If you knew you had a month to live, would you do anything differently? Would it change your mind about your priorities?

I've seen a graph before that shows you can find your purpose at the intersection of:

1. What you enjoy (we all have a passion)
2. What you're good at (explore your talents)
3. Something people value (what would people pay you for?)

So, where do you have skills, what do you enjoy, and what do people value in you?

Some people have a very difficult time with this, and I'll explain why that's okay. See, people struggle because they've been doing what other people want them to do, not what they think they should be doing themselves. Some people, like Tim, get it right away. For others, they're still looking.

Don't get me wrong. If you're in a dire situation with no food or electricity, then you're probably just looking for a meal and to turn the lights on. So, if you're even in a position to ask yourself what your purpose is, then you're ahead of most of humanity. Be glad.

Throughout this book, I've questioned the self-help gurus from the past, and I'll do that again now. Here's the harsh truth:

Maybe the question never goes away. Maybe the question of your life's purpose never gets answered.

Even if you do find something you're good at and other people value and you really enjoy doing... things change. Nothing will be the same in 5 or 10 years. Circumstances change, man. Life changes. The world changes.

"So what do we do, Matt?" you may be wondering.

The key to all this is realizing that things do change, and that you don't have to answer the question once and for all. The key is to consistently be asking yourself the question:

Where is the most important place for me to put my time today? That's the Daily Question.

It's part of the Daily Climb.

PRINCIPLE
10

MY EULOGY

OR

Something's Gonna Get You; Leave a Legacy; Keep the End in Mind, Nobody Lives Forever; Face the Facts

Picture this:

You're at a party, and it's a good one. Your buddies are there, they're serving the kind of drinks that you like, the music is hitting just right, and even though you aren't usually the sort of person to notice the decorations – hell, even those are pretty awesome.

But then you get a tap on the shoulder. You have somewhere else to be, and it's time to go. The party is going to go on without you. Some of your friends and others you know will still be there, and you wish you could be too.

But you can't. And that stinks.

So, the question becomes, do you have anything you need to leave behind for those who are still enjoying the party? Did you make it a better party while you were there, or did you get distracted and just miss out? Did you make a difference? Did you make things better with your presence? Could you have done more?

What kind of an impact will you leave behind?

Alright, you can stop imagining that party now. We're back here in real life, but it isn't all that different. Even if you've got a great life and are enjoying it, God's going to tap you on the shoulder one day and say, "Hey, Buddy. Your time is done down here." But life is going to go on without you.

Or maybe life, to you, is anything but a party. Maybe it's a drag. Maybe you just keep hoping it'll get better. Will you ever get around to living a fulfilling life? Something that you're actually excited about?

For whatever else it is, this game of life has a time limit. And you're closer to the end now than when you started reading this book.

Remember the pennies story from the foreword? My friend Phillip had a friend of his break out a roll of one hundred pennies and remove 58 (for how old he was), and then he took away another 15 (assuming he'd live to 85), and then he took away 5 more (on the assumption those last 5 years he might not be very active or able.) Looking at how many pennies he had left changed Phillip's mindset that day, and when he told me the story, it changed mine, too.

I'm not going to get philosophical on you – the lesson is just recognizing how many years you probably have left, if all goes well. You can't really affect change if you don't know the score of the game.

Knowing the score has always been important to me. You must know the score in business, with your health and in life. When I do this exercise, it still makes me stop and refocus on my priorities.

I'm 50 years old now, so that's half the pennies. My mom's dad died young, so that's in the family history. My other grandfather died at 88. My parents are still alive.

I've already had a joint replacement, and I have a lot of arthritis. I'll be hurting, but let's say all goes well and I live into my eighties. I've got a little over 30 to go.

I don't want to waste those thirty pennies. There are ways I can protect them and make sure I don't lose any. But no matter how successful in business I can be, or how many friends I have, or how many goals I accomplish – I can't earn any extras, and neither can you.

In the old days, they didn't discuss politics or religion in polite company. Today, we don't talk about death. If you bring it up, people will get uncomfortable, look at you funny, and think, "He's rude." Strange, considering it's just a fact of life.

It isn't something most of us like to think about, but I've got news for you:

You are going to die.

Every one of us is terminal. It's going to happen to all of us, eventually, so we might as well talk about it.

Inevitable things should be planned for. Death may not seem relevant to you if you're still 19 and invincible, If you're 40, 60, 75... let's just say that fact becomes increasingly relevant.

And yes, recognizing all this does have religious implications, and you should figure that out – but that isn't where I'm going with all this.

What will you have done with your time on this earth when it's all over?

What will people say at your funeral?

When I was a teenager, my father's friend tragically passed away in an airplane crash. At the funeral, Pastor Larry Williams got up in front of the crowd at Ooltewah Baptist and said, "It's not my place to remember Paul's life. It's yours."

Then, he just sat down.

There were two microphones on stage, and it didn't take long for people to start lining up to share memories about the departed and telling stories about ways he'd helped people that even his family hadn't been aware of. Paul was a good man. We celebrated his life that day.

That stuck with me my whole life, and I've never forgotten it.

That's why, when it's my time to go, I'll be speaking at my own funeral.

No, I don't mean anything crazy or woo-woo. I mean that I'd rather decide what my eulogy says than make one of my friends stumble through writing something while they're grieving.

At my funeral, someone will read the eulogy that I wrote, and then we'll have those two microphones on stage, so that people can just get up and celebrate Matt.

This isn't morbid, it's just being honest with the facts, and taking them into account. It's everything this book has been talking about so far: having a vision, setting your priorities and mindset, finding the right guide and tribe to help get you there, and making that daily climb every time you get out of bed. Writing your own eulogy just makes it so that you can know what you're working towards.

Begin with the end in mind, they say.

So, without any more beating around the bush, this is what you'll hear if you attend my funeral some day:

> Thank you for being here, and I'm sorry. I loved each and every one of you... possibly, depending on who's here, but probably 99% of you. If there is one here that I didn't love, y'all probably know who it is and they're feeling pretty awkward right now.

> Some might think writing your own eulogy is morbid. I didn't. I'd rather tell you about me than make someone else do it. I know how I felt, and I know I had a vision that hopefully I've now accomplished.

> I had successes and accomplishments, won awards, built businesses, sat on a bunch of boards and all that, but that's not what I want my legacy to be. I want you to remember me for being a good

friend, a good spouse, a good father, a witness to others, and someone who always wanted to make things better.

I repeatedly thought about how to make things better. I repeatedly thought about the things I wanted in life. I knew I was born to be somebody and fulfill my dreams. I knew I could do something great with my life and expected great things to come. I looked for the blessing, not the curse. I focused on the positive, not the negative.

I wasn't ashamed of my Christian faith. Many of you have held hands and prayed with me at the dinner table. I laughed and I cried with you, but today is a celebration. This is not a sermon, but I will say if you're not saved, you're missing out. I'm walking on gold streets with my friends and family that beat me here. I can't imagine hell. That'd suck and you'd be stupid to go there.

I loved my wife Jenny so deeply. I enjoyed our vacations, our walks, her healthy cooking, her love for our family, and I really enjoyed our alone time, wink. Jenny was truly my soulmate. Don't quit being Jenny because I'm not here anymore, angel. I'm still with you. Be happy. I know we're not done yet and will see you again. You count on it.

I'll never forget when my daughter Reese was born, then driving her to school, all the hugs goodnight, her graduation, and so many fun times together. I had the sweetest and most amazing human for a daughter that anyone could have. I was so blessed to be part of her life. You keep it up Reese. You were the light of my life. Still are. Be your best.

I lived a life full of adventure and had the best damn friends any guy could have.

I caught 30" rainbow trout in Alaska fly fishing next to a 900-pound brown bear.

I killed a 300-pound, 14-point whitetail buck in the Upper Peninsula with my great friend Tim.

I watched the sunrise over Reelfoot Lake with Dr. Dave slaying ducks with my Benelli shotgun. Jenny, give it to Reese's husband.

I went camping with my newlywed at Wig Meadow, hiked the Tetons, and we jumped in Jenny Lake next to the Rockefeller's cabin.

I went snow skiing in 5 states, went whale watching in Cabo, and watched my daughter surf the waves in Maui.

In my second half of life, I traveled the world with Jenny, and we had a blast. I helped grow companies and either raised or gave millions to charities and non-profits. I've been called a "Difference Maker," and I was proud of that.

I visited dozens of islands, visited nearly every state, and went gambling at the Monte Carlo Casino.

I played some of the world's best golf courses and played a hand in building a couple of them.

I went to Augusta National, the Final Four, UT's National Championship game in the same town I'd own a restaurant 25 years later. I went to Super Bowl 50 and Peyton's after party.

Man, I lived.

I watched multiple goal posts come down at Neyland Stadium, the stadium I've also made love in. Ladies' bathroom, section QQ.

I drank the world's finest wines and Uncle Bob's moonshine.

I saw everything from a Kid Rock concert to Broadway plays and hung out on Charlie Daniel's and Merle Haggard's tour buses.

I rode the Cannonball at Lake Winnie. My best friend had the same last name.

I ran naked in the snow and danced with my wife in the rain.

Man, I lived.

I flew on the back of planes and co-piloted my own.

I won some races and I lost some races, and all of them had a purpose.

Along the way what I can tell you is from Buds on Brainerd Road to the Country Club, the beer tastes the same.

So if I'm 50 or 95 when the big man checks me in, just know this:

That Matt lived... and lived he did.

I enjoyed connecting and helping people, and

hopefully I've done that along the way for you. I hope now I'm being remembered for being that "difference maker."

I wrote a book when I was 50, The Daily Climb. If you haven't read it, there are copies in the back on your way out.

One of the best funerals I attended, the preacher didn't spend time remembering the guy's life. He put 2 microphones on stage and the guests lined up to tell stories and celebrate. It's your job to remember me. I know you have a story to tell, so start lining up.

I Love you and "insist" you live your life with purpose, and make sure you're coming to Heaven to see me. As my dad always said, "Save your fork, the best is yet to come."

So what's the point of all this? It's the end of the book. As I'm writing this, it is my 50th birthday, my daughter just graduated from high school, I'm beginning a new venture in the country music and e-commerce industry, and, like you, I'm trying to figure out how it all goes together. And this is what I've come up with:

If I could do it all over again, I'd do it with these ten principles from the beginning. I'd have stressed myself out less, simplified more, and been more focused on what matters. I've learned a few things along the way, but I can't have a do-over. Those pennies are already spent, and I'm not getting them back. For better and for worse, I've bought what I've bought with my time, and now there's only what's left.

But what's left matters a lot. And the second chance we all get is each morning when the sun rises. Today can be the start of something new, as we keep chasing that hero vision of ourselves a few years down the road.

Truth is, life isn't always a party. It's a grind. It's a climb. Nobody's promised tomorrow, and a lot of the time it's two steps forward one step back – even at our best.

But all that just makes the good stuff all the more rare and valuable. If I always wanted to accomplish something, it'd be a shame not to get around to it. (That's why I'm going to learn how to play that damn guitar.)

I hope I leave a legacy, not of businesses created or money made or material things or status, but of loving the people that God put in my life, fulfilling my purpose, and enjoying the ride.

So this book ends the way my life will, and it ends the way your life will, too. With a funeral.

But may that funeral have two very long lines in front of those microphones, with plenty of laughs, good stories, and grateful people who you helped.

Everybody dies. Not everybody lives.

Life's a one lap race and you're still on the track.

So get up in the morning, even if it hurts, work into those extra big shoes, do what it takes to be just a little bit better every day, and you might as well smile as you do.

That's the daily climb.

ABOUT THE AUTHOR

Matt Hullander is an entrepreneur from Chattanooga, Tennessee, with business interests in Tennessee, Florida, Alabama, Ohio, and Arizona, ranging from real estate development, private equity, and e-commerce. Matt grew his primary business to become one of the largest exterior remodeling companies in the country before selling the business in 2021. Matt was chosen as Businessman of the Year in Chattanooga by Cityscope Magazine. Replacement Contractor Magazine named Matt "Contractor of the Year." Matt's company received several awards, including the Chattanooga Chamber's "Small Business of the Year," The BBB's "Torch Award for Business Place Ethics" (twice), and Matt was inducted into Remodeling Magazine's "Big 50."

Matt is a partner with Scenic Land Company, a real estate development company best known for their resort development in north Georgia called McLemore. Matt's other companies include V2 Strategy, V2 Ventures, V2 Properties, V2 Aviation, Thompson 105 Restaurant, Cult Coffee, Orange Rhino Concrete Coatings, Legacy Dental Group, and his most recent venture, Nashville Grind. Nashville Grind is an e-commerce company run by Matt and a collective of singers and songwriters to promote products while giving proceeds back to help others.

Matt has served on several business and charity boards, and he currently sits on the board for First Horizon Bank. Matt has been a featured speaker at industry events and a guest on several podcasts. Matt is known as a connector, always willing to help others with a focus on vision and mindset.

Matt shares a daily motivational email and is the author of his book, The Daily Climb. To learn more visit MattHullander.com

V2 is an aviation term meaning the speed at which the airplane will climb. At this speed the aircraft is committed to take off. Matt enjoys helping individuals and businesses reach their potential and climb.

AUTHORS' POINT OF CONTACT
MATT HULLANDER

- matthullander.com

- **f** @matthullander

- **in** linkedin.com/in/matthullander

- @matt_hullander

- @matt_hullander

NOTES

i.   DeBoer, Mick. "19 Mind-Blowing New Year's Resolution Statistics" A meta-data analysis and summary of studies and articles that he lists under "resources" at the bottom of the page. Nov. 15, 2022.
https://insideoutmastery.com/new-years-resolution-statistics/

ii.   Runge, Marschall. M.D., Ph.D. "Weighing the Facts: the Tough Truth about Weight Loss" April 12, 2017. University of Michigan Medicine.
https://www.michiganmedicine.org/health-lab/
weighing-facts-tough-truth-about-weight-loss

iii.   Keynes, John Maynard. "Economic Possibilities for our Grandchildren." *Nation and Athenaeum*, October 11 and 18, 1930.
https://www.aspeninstitute.org/wp-content/uploads/files/content/upload/Intro_and_Section_I.pdf

iv.   McCollum, Parker. "Handle on You," Track 6 on "Never Enough." MCA Nashville, August 15, 2022

v.   McKeown, Greg. *Essentialism: the Disciplined Pursuit of Less.* Currency Publishing, April 15, 2014. From Chapter 1.

vi.   *https://elitecontentmarketer.com/screen-time-statistics/*

vii.   This is a quote from The E-Myth by Michael Gerber. If you're a business owner, you ought to read it.

viii.   *https://www.nytimes.com/2011/10/23/technology/at-waldorf-school-in-silicon-valley-technology-can-wait.html*

ix.   *www.ilovecult.com* to order his coffee. Shameless plug.

x.   *www.NashvilleGrind.com.*

xi.   Luke 12:48b, NKJV

xii.   Luke 21:1-4

xiii.   Eppley, Ed and Burke, Adrienne. Let's Be Clear: 6 Disciplines of Focused Management Pros Jan. 29, 2018.

xiv.   The Eppley Experience

xv.   Almberg, Cross, Dobson, Smith, Metz, Stahler, and Hudson. "Social Living Mitigates the Costs of a Chronic Illness in a Cooperative Carnivore." *Ecology Letters.* May 18, 2015.
https://onlinelibrary.wiley.com/doi/10.1111/ele.12444/abstract;jsessionid=0B5EF2AECB4B29A23AEEC5109DB21974.f02t02

xvi.   I would be remiss if I did not mention that many of the ideas of how to set up a tribe that I relate in this chapter come from a good book called Tribe of Millionaires by Mike MCarthy and Pat Hiban. It's worth the read, and they have some great resources on their website.

xvii.   Azab, Marwa Ph.D. "Why Sharing Your Goals Makes Them Less Acheivable" *Psychology Today*, Jan. 1, 2018.
https://www.psychologytoday.com/us/blog/neuroscience-in-everyday-life/201801/why-sharing-your-goals-makes-them-less-achievable

Printed in the USA
CPSIA information can be obtained
at www.ICGtesting.com
JSHW012226270823
47206JS00005B/11